PRINCIPLES *of* HARMONIC ANALYSIS

RESPECTFULLY DEDICATED TO

NADIA BOULANGER

By Walter Piston

Orchestral Works

Symphonic Piece	1927
Suite for Orchestra	1929
Concerto for Orchestra	1933
Prelude and Fugue for Orchestra	1937
Symphony	1937
Ballet — "The Incredible Flutist"	1938

Chamber Music

Three Pieces for Flute, Clarinet and Bassoon	1926
Sonata for Flute and Piano	1930
Suite for Oboe and Piano	1931
String Quartet No. 1	1933
String Quartet No. 2	1935
Trio for Violin, Cello and Pianoforte	1935

Chamber Orchestra

Concertino for Pianoforte and Chamber Orchestra	1937

Theoretical Works

°Principles of Harmonic Analysis	1933

°*Second Printing* 1938
°*Third Printing* 1941
°*Fourth Printing* 1944
°*Fifth Printing* 1946
°*Sixth Printing* 1950
°*Seventh Printing* 1959

Harmony	1941

PRINCIPLES *of* HARMONIC ANALYSIS

WALTER PISTON
Assistant Professor of Music at Harvard University

BOSTON
E. C. SCHIRMER MUSIC CO.
1933
All rights reserved

Copyright, 1933,
BY
E. C. SCHIRMER MUSIC CO.
For all countries

RESPECTFULLY DEDICATED TO
NADIA BOULANGER

INTRODUCTION

The technical study of the diversified and apparently unrelated idioms of twentieth century composers is most logically approached through a clear conception of what harmonic practice has been throughout the preceding two hundred years. Musical theory being made up of deductions arrived at by observing the common practice of composers over a long time, it is plain that the formulation of such theory will be difficult in a period when almost no common practice can be detected. The vast amount of individual practice to be observed since 1900 may be sorted out to some extent and classified, but this is most satisfactorily accomplished by reference to certain trends or departures from accepted standards. It has then become increasingly important that the standard or point of departure should be made as clear as possible. One must not lose sight of the fact, however, that in defining such a standard we are not asserting truth so much as outlining a hypothesis, worthwhile only as long as it is useful, and which will undoubtedly be remade as the years furnish a more simplifying perspective.

The purpose of this book is not to pursue an immediate investigation of contemporary harmonic technique, but to help lay the foundation for this investigation by clarifying accepted theory and showing what the common practice of composers has been. It must be understood that this common practice is necessarily departed from by all composers, if they are to possess individuality. The so-called "rules" of harmony represent what is done by all and hence might be termed the platitudes of music. If we speak of rules being broken by Bach and Beethoven, we are strengthening the popular misconception that the rules were made for composers to follow, whereas the process is just the opposite.

The actual first-hand study of the works of composers, as a means of discovering their procedure, is far superior to the reading of books, technical or otherwise, about music. This simple truth is the excuse, if any is needed, for advocating the systematic study of harmonic analysis, since to get at the fundamental harmony it is necessary to go deeply into the counterpoint, rhythm, instrumental figuration, and other stylistic elements which make up the great difference in externals between music and harmony exercises.

Harmonic analysis is more than a description of chords as individuals. In its broader aspects it is a process involving a study of the shape, proportions, and underlying skeleton of a piece of music, as well as its more superficial texture. It is indispensable to the student of any branch of music. It should be begun simultaneously with the study of harmony, where it will be found helpful in avoiding the confusion in

INTRODUCTION

the student's mind between the writing of harmony exercises and the composing of music. By showing how every composer departs from common practice, it will serve to demonstrate the real value of harmony exercises in the scheme; i.e., that of helping to establish the norm or standard by the practical application of procedure common to all. If this philosophical result is accomplished, and if a solid foundation is established for a closer insight into the music of the past and present, the aim of this book will be attained.

WALTER PISTON

Belmont, Massachusetts
July, 1932

CONTENTS

		PAGE
INTRODUCTION		v
CHAPTER ONE	Harmonic Material	1
CHAPTER TWO	Contrapuntal Material	30
CHAPTER THREE	Modulation	39
CHAPTER FOUR	The Twentieth Century	48
APPENDIX	Examples of Complete Harmonic Analysis of Pieces	53
INDEX		90

PRINCIPLES OF HARMONIC ANALYSIS

CHAPTER ONE

Harmonic Material

The most important observation about a given chord does not concern its make-up as regards intervals between the notes, etc., but rather what its relation is to the rest of the music. In other words, it is far less significant that a chord happens to be, for example, a major or a minor triad than that it happens to be a tonic or a sub-dominant chord. It is therefore necessary that each chord be given a label which shows the scale degree of its root, and incidentally its tonality. The system of Roman numerals seems to be as good as any, besides having the advantage of being in general use. In view of the large number of different chords having the same scale degree as a root, and consequently the same Roman numeral, it has been thought advisable to abandon the system of varying the size of the numeral according to the kind of intervals in the chord.

When Arabic numerals are used in this book, they refer to intervals formed between the bass note and other factors of the chord, as, for example, six, five, three, for the first inversion of a seventh chord.

The following comprehensive list contains the forms of the chords on each scale degree, and is to be considered as the vocabulary of chords in common use. It is true that other chromatic alterations exist, but they should be regarded as, and will be seen to be, exceptions. These exceptions are in some cases personal or national mannerisms and in other cases may be called "modernisms." They are not to be regarded as mistakes on the part of the composer or instances of "rule-breaking," but as departures from common practice, the discovery of which is an instructive and interesting by-product of the process of harmonic analysis.

There is enough difference of opinion among theorists to warrant a statement here that chords constructed upon the leading-tone will be considered dominants without root, except as otherwise indicated. Dominant chords without root are indicated by the sign V⁰.

Any degree of the scale, major or minor, (with the exception of the leading-tone, a purely melodic note) may be preceded by its dominant without disturbing the tonality. That is, a dominant seventh chord constructed on the first degree would be the dominant of the fourth degree and hence should be called V of IV. This dominant harmony may take any of the forms shown below under "Chords on the dominant," with or without root, and may even have an irregular resolution, for instance to II. It is hoped that this important principle will be made clear by the examples given.

In the following list, each chord is first presented as it would stand in the key of C, and then shown in natural surroundings in an example from musical literature. The examples have been chosen from as wide and varied a field as possible and the reader is urged to seek further examples of each chord. It is also desirable that the actual compositions should be consulted in every case so that the chord may be seen and heard in its entire context.

Chords on the Tonic

The difference between the major and minor modes with the same tonic reduces itself to a question of whether there is a preponderance of the major or minor third degree. The minor sixth degree (A-flat in the key of C) cannot be said to indicate the mode, since it appears so often in the major mode, especially during the nineteenth century. In fact, the two modes become practically interchangeable when the style is somewhat chromatic.

HARMONIC MATERIAL

Ex. 2.

HÄNDEL
Suite for Harpsichord

G: VI　II$_6^5$　V　I$_6^5$　IV　VII$_6^5$　III　VI$_6^5$　II　V$_7$　I

Ex. 3.

BRAHMS. Op 117, No. 2
Intermezzo

B♭: I$_6$　I$_7$　IV$_7$　V$_7$ of III

This chord is usually explainable as a plain triad with the seventh a non-harmonic tone resolving to the octave, and is for this reason not admitted as a chord by many theorists.

Ex. 4.

WAGNER
"Die Meistersinger" (Act I)

G: V$_{\frac{4}{3}}$ of V　V$_7$　I$_7$　V$_7$ of V　V$_7$

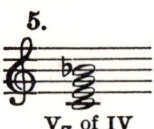

This shows clearly the use of the dominant of the sub-dominant as a factor in establishing the key of C. To say that the movement starts in F is to attribute undue power to the single note B-flat.

Ninth chords are found usually in dominant form on all degrees, except in music of a later period than that we are studying here. When they are not dominants, such chords are best analyzed as containing non-harmonic tones.

Seventh and ninth chords with augmented fifth may be considered "modernisms" in relation to the present theory. The raised fifth first appears in the dominant chords and is common enough to be included in the vocabulary.

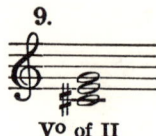

The root of this chord is really VI. Dominants without root may conveniently be indicated by V^o.

Same as the above with seventh added, making a dominant minor ninth with root missing. The ninth of V of II is normally minor, since the major ninth would not make an appropriate dominant to a minor tonic.

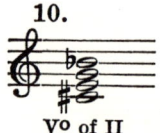

HARMONIC MATERIAL

The tonic triad is seldom found in this form, except when the g-sharp occurs as a passing-tone between g-natural and a.

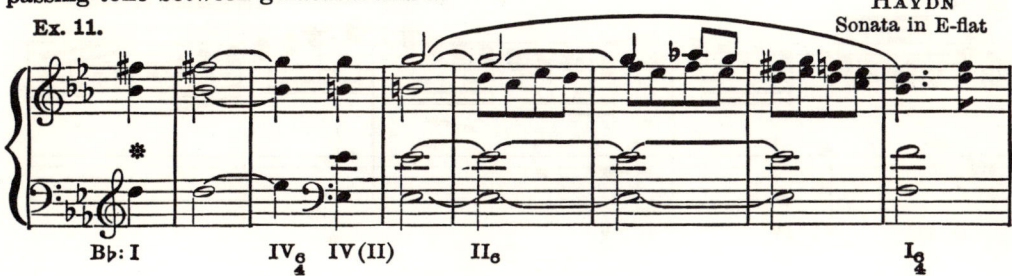

Chords on the Supertonic

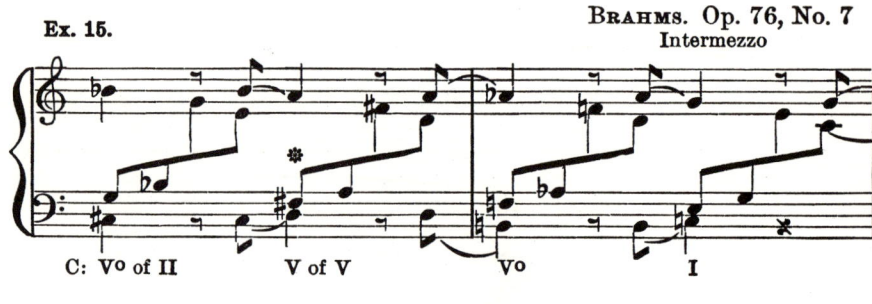

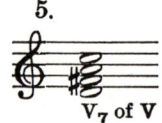

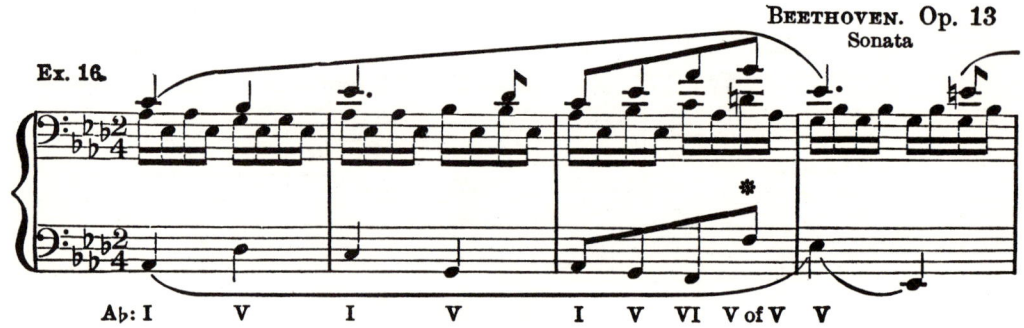

HARMONIC MATERIAL

6. V_9 of V

Ex. 17. FRANCK
Symphonic Variations

A: V_9 of V V_9 I

7. V_9 of V

Ex. 18. FRANCK
Symphony

B♭: IV   I = G: III   V°   I$^6_4$ V° of VI   VI$^6_4$ I V_9 of V   V

8. II$_9$

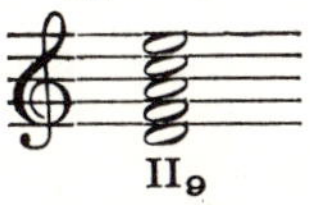

The ninth of this chord practically always resolves to the second degree before the chord proceeds to V. (See the remark under chord No. 6 on the tonic.)

Ex. 19. GRIEG. Op. 7
Sonata

C: II$_9$ V$_7$ I

10   PRINCIPLES OF HARMONIC ANALYSIS

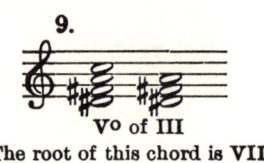

The root of this chord is VII

When this chord is used to introduce the tonic triad it is not to be considered as V of III with missing root, but as a seventh chord on the second degree with root and third raised.

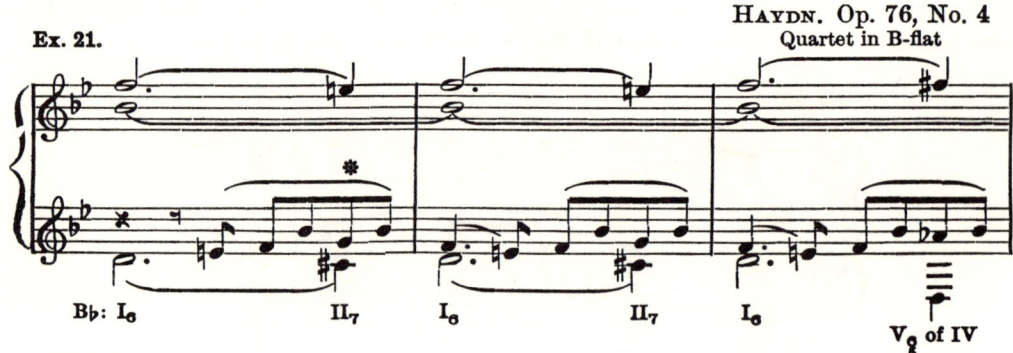

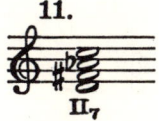

This chord is most often found with its fifth in the bass making the "augmented six-four-three" chord.

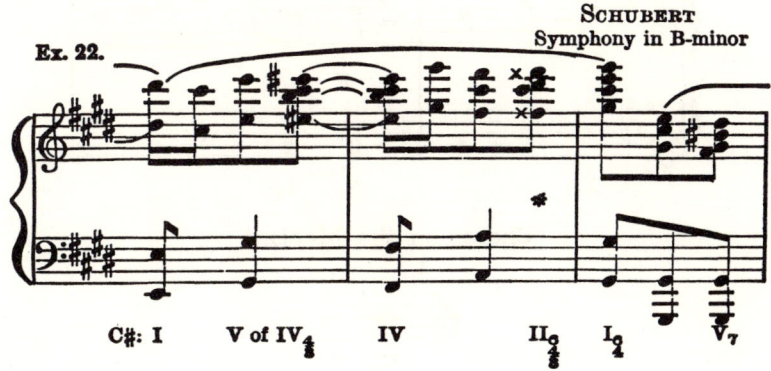

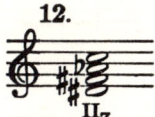

When its fifth is in the bass, this chord makes what is called the "chord of the doubly augmented fourth" and usually proceeds to a major tonic six-four chord.

13.

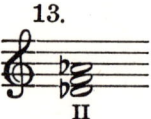

Almost always found in the first inversion, this chord is known as the "Neapolitan sixth" and might conveniently be indicated by the sign N_6.

Chords on the Mediant

1.

2.

HARMONIC MATERIAL

HARMONIC MATERIAL

Since the sixth degree of C may be either a-natural or a-flat, dominants on e-natural and e-flat are both possible.

Chords on the Subdominant

1.

Ex. 36.

WAGNER
"Das Rheingold" (Scene II)

2.

Ex. 37.

MOZART
Adagio

3.

Ex. 38.

SCHUMANN
Valse Noble

HARMONIC MATERIAL

HARMONIC MATERIAL

Usually with its third in the bass; the "augmented sixth" chord.

Usually with its third in the bass; the "augmented six-five-three."

Not uncommon, however, in root position.

12.

IV

The augmented triad on the fourth degree nearly always proves to be the supertonic triad with a chromatic appoggiatura.

Ex. 48.   HAYDN
Sonata in E-flat

E♭: IV   II₆   I₆₄

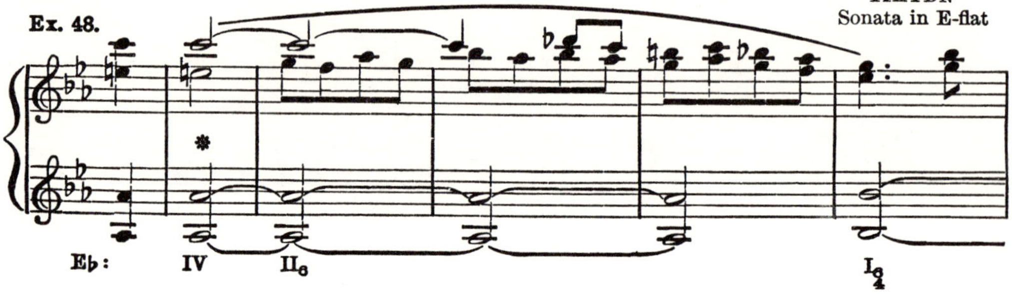

Chords on the Dominant

1.

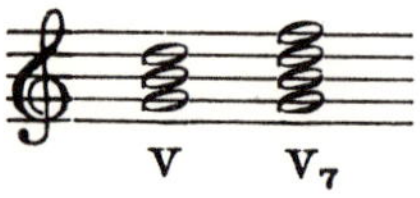

V   V₇

Ex. 49.   BEETHOVEN. Op. 2, No. 2
Sonata

A: V₇ —————————————————— I —

2.

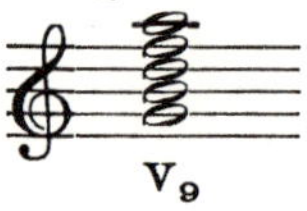

V₉

Ex. 50.   FRANCK
Sonata for Violin and Piano

A: V₉   (II)   V₉   I

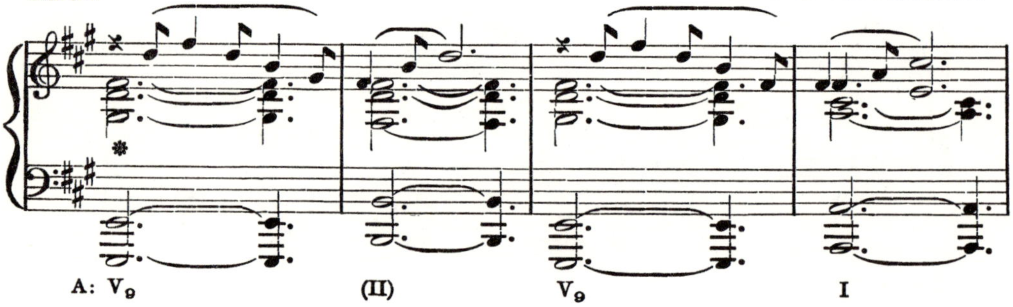

HARMONIC MATERIAL

Ex. 51. Schumann — Symphonic Studies

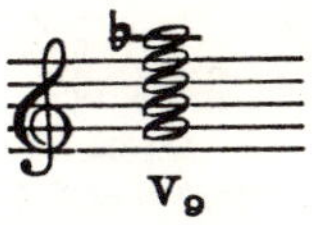

C♯: V₉ ——————————————— I⁶₄

Ex. 52. Lalo — Spanish Symphony

D: I   V⁷₆   I   V⁷₆   I   V/I   I

This form is sometimes found when the descending melodic-minor scale is used.

Ex. 53. D. Scarlatti — Sonata

D: I   V   I   V   IV   II

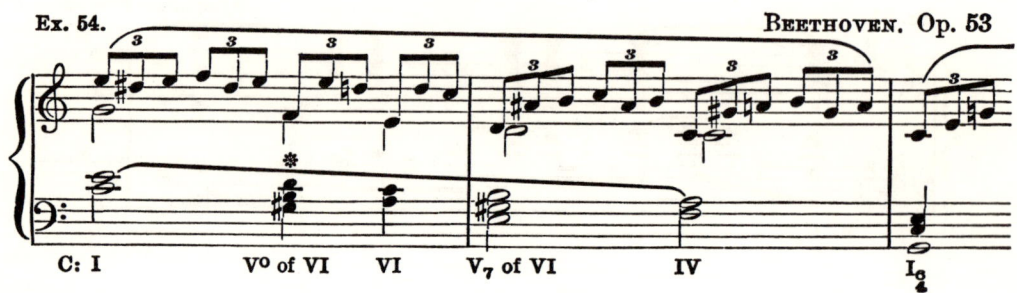

New alterations are more likely to appear in connection with dominant harmony than in chords on other degrees of the scale. Hence we find, toward the latter part of the period of common practice, that the dominant seventh chord with augmented fifth is used often enough to be cited among the chords employed by composers, although such a chord was not a part of the harmonic idiom in the classical or early romantic periods. The dominant major ninth chord with raised fifth is still more to be considered a "modern" chord. These chords form a convenient link between the procedure we are studying here and the practice of later composers, such as Debussy and Ravel, and their followers.

HARMONIC MATERIAL

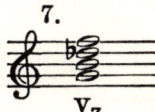

The lowered fifth is even more uncommon than the augmented fifth, except when it occurs in the bass, when it forms the "augmented six-four-three" chord. It will be noted, however, that this chord has a strong tendency to cause its chord of resolution to sound more like a dominant than a tonic, unless other strong chords are present to stabilize the tonality.

Chords on the Submediant

24   PRINCIPLES OF HARMONIC ANALYSIS

2.

VI_7

Ex. 58.
PURCELL
Suite

C: VII   III VI_7 II_7 V   I

3.

VI

Ex. 59.
BRAHMS
Symphony No. 3

C: I   VI   I   VI   IV   I

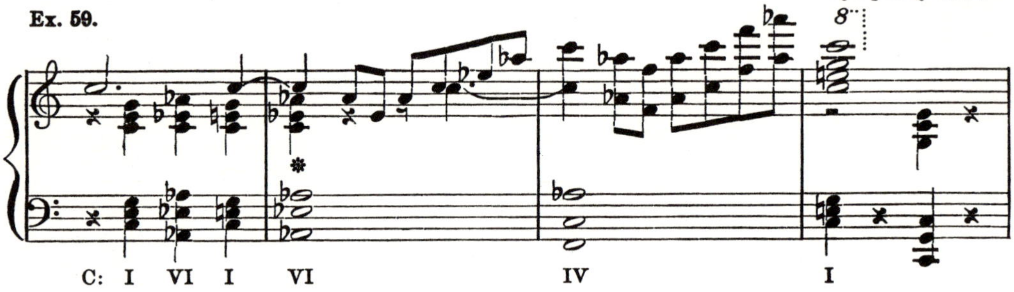

4.

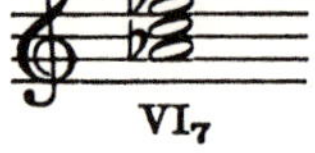

VI_7

Ex. 60.
WAGNER
"Götterdämmerung" (Act. III)

G: VI_7 VI_7 V

HARMONIC MATERIAL

5.

VI_7

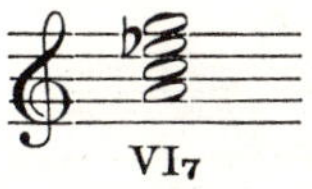

In this form the minor third degree is found in combination with the major sixth degree. This is usually the result of the use of the ascending melodic-minor scale, although in the following example the raised sixth degree descends.

Ex. 61.
RAMEAU
Sarabande
(From Suite No. 6)

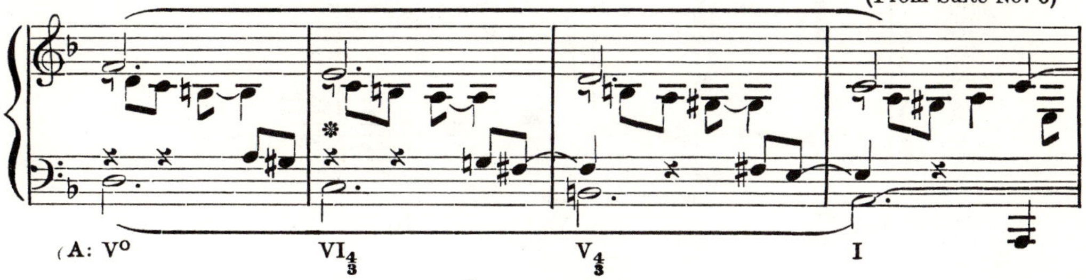

(A: V^o) $VI_{\frac{4}{3}}$ $V_{\frac{4}{3}}$ I

6.

V of II

Ex. 62.
SCHUMANN. Op. 19
Blumenstück

Db: V^o of II   II   V of II II_6 $V_{\frac{6}{5}}$ of V   V $V_{\frac{6}{4}}$ of V $V_{\frac{6}{5}}$

7.

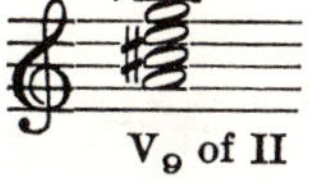

V_9 of II

Ex. 63.
SCHUBERT
Sonata in B-flat

Bb: V_9 of II   II   V   I

Usually used to introduce some form of V.

This chord is sometimes used before the "Neapolitan sixth" and might be called V of N_6.

Chords on the Seventh Degree

1.

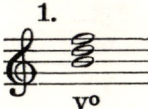

Best considered V, except perhaps in stepwise progressions like the following:

2.

Nearly always a dominant ninth without root. This chord is a real VII when it moves to III, a somewhat unusual progression, except in sequences.

HARMONIC MATERIAL

6.

VII

Sometimes occurs as a result of the use of the descending melodic-minor scale.

Ex. 73.
MATTHESON
Air from Suite No. 5

C: V　I₆　VII₆　VI₆　V₆　I　IV₆　—　V

7.

V of III

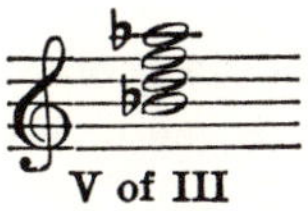

Ex. 74.
SCHUMANN
3rd Symphony

E♭: I　VI　II₆/5　V₇　I　V of III　III　V₇ of IV　IV　II　V₆/5　V of IV　IV　I₆　V₇ of V　IV₆

8.

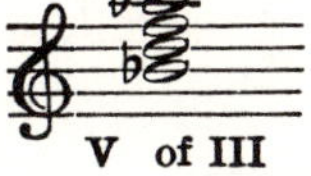

V of III

Ex. 75.
MOUSSORGSKY
Death's Serenade

E♭: I　II₆　I　VII (V₉ of III)　III　(V)

CHAPTER TWO

Contrapuntal Material

The independent rhythmic and melodic movement of the various parts or voices in music is made possible largely by the use of so-called non-harmonic tones, that is, tones which are not a part of the chord with which they are heard. Historically, the chords themselves are the result of simultaneous sounding of melodic parts, but over two hundred years of harmonic or vertical hearing have led us to believe that the chord is the more elementary factor, with the counterpoint superposed. Composers of the twentieth century have in many cases endeavored to return to the contrapuntal or horizontal point of view, even going to the extreme of abandoning any principles of interval between the voices. This naturally produces a music very difficult to listen to from the harmonic standpoint, but which often possesses an organic life and freedom much to be desired.

Since the present study is one of the harmonic structure it is necessary to classify and relate these non-harmonic tones with reference to the accompanying harmony.

1. The Passing-tone

Passing-tones are tones which fill the space between two different harmonic tones not necessarily members of the same chord. This interval will be either a third, fourth or second and may be bridged diatonically or chromatically, or by a combination of both, as long as the melodic progression contains no skip.

Although passing tones may occur on the beat, or simultaneously with a change of harmony, it is inaccurate to speak of an "accented passing-tone." All passing-tones are unaccented unless they are purposely given an artificial accent. The so-called "accented passing-tone" is more correctly classified as an appoggiatura. (See below.)

× = *passing-tone on the beat*

2. The Appoggiatura

As its Italian name implies (*appoggiare* — to lean), the appoggiatura is distinguished by its rhythmic stress, or melodic weight. It appears on the beat, most effectively with a change of harmony. It may enter by skip, step or repetition, and resolves by step up or down, to a note of the chord. In the following example, it is the first note of an entering voice.

× = *appoggiatura*

× = *appoggiatura entering by step*

A comparison of the above example with the example given of the passing-tone on the beat will show the importance of the rhythmic stress.

The appoggiatura entering by repetition should not be confused with the suspension. Here the distinction is of great importance as the two interpretations are widely different in rhythm and style.

Ex. 81. BEETHOVEN. Op. 8
Trio for Violin, Viola and 'Cello

D: I   V$_{\frac{4}{3}}$ I   V   I

×= *appoggiatura entering by repetition*

3. The Suspension

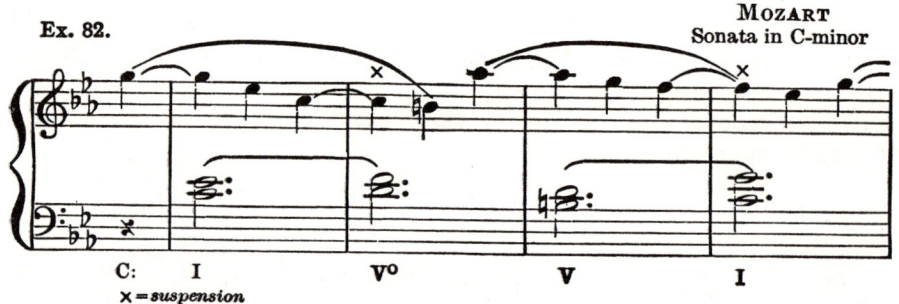

Ex. 82. MOZART
Sonata in C-minor

C: I   V°   V   I

×= *suspension*

The characteristic of the suspension is the tied note, displacing the bar-line for the part involved and thus giving it the added interest of an independent rhythm. The suspension usually resolves down by step to a note of the chord, but may also have an upward resolution.

Ex. 83. SCHUMANN
Figured Choral

F: IV   VII$_{\frac{6}{4}}$ I$_{\frac{6}{4}}$ IV$_6$ V$_{\frac{9}{8}}$ I

×= *suspension with upward resolution*

Sometimes the resolution is accompanied by a change of harmony.

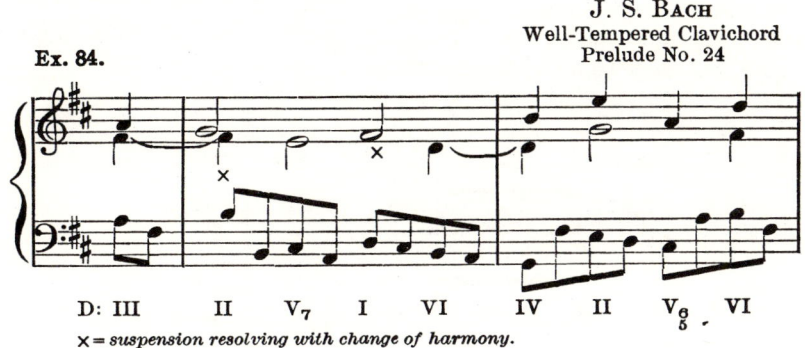

× = *suspension resolving with change of harmony.*

The resolution of a suspension is susceptible to various ornamentations. The most common of these ornaments are the échappée and the *cambiata*, explained below.
Echappée between suspension and note of resolution.

× = *échappée*

Cambiata between suspension and note of resolution.

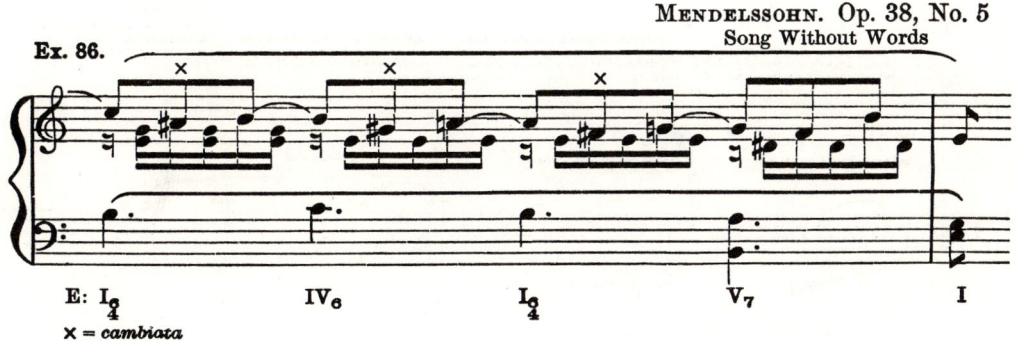

× = *cambiata*

4. The Échappée

In its usual form the échappée leaves a note by step and then proceeds by a skip of a third in the opposite direction. The first note may be a harmony note or a non-harmonic tone, such as the suspension or appoggiatura. The note following is usually a harmony note, but may be an appoggiatura or a cambiata.

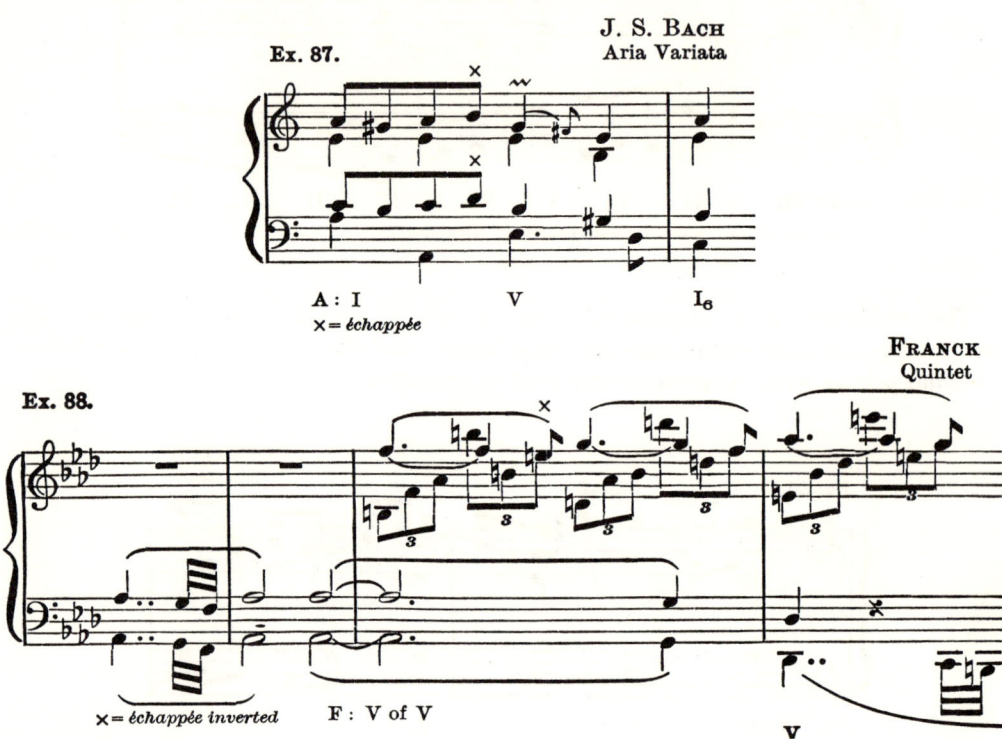

Larger skips than that of a third may be found, this being very often the result of the interpolation of an appoggiatura.

5. The Cambiata

This is the reverse of the preceding. The cambiata enters by a skip of a third and resolves by step in the opposite direction. It will be seen that both the cambiata and the échappée are employed as weak or unaccented rhythmic factors, and in each case are found between two notes a second apart, either just before a change of harmony, or between a dissonance and its resolution.

6. The Auxiliary Tone

The auxiliary tone is likewise weak rhythmically. It leaves a harmony note by step and returns to the same note. It may be either above or below and may be diatonic or chromatic.

The double auxiliary may be likened to a five note turn with the third note omitted or to a combination in which the *échappée* proceeds to a cambiata.

Ex. 93. Chopin. Op. 25, No. 7
Etude

E: II⁶₅   I⁶₄

×× = *double auxiliary tones*

7. The Anticipation

This term explains itself. It is applied to a note which arrives too soon, that is, before the harmony changes. It is usually shorter than the note it anticipates and in most cases the note is repeated when the chord changes, rather than being tied.

Ex. 94. Händel
Concerto Grosso in D-minor

D: II   V   I

× = *anticipation*

8. The Pedal

Originally this term referred to the practice of organists of holding down a pedal note through various harmonies, and is sometimes called organ-point or pedal-point. In actual practice it may occur in any register. To be a real pedal, it should at some moment be combined with a chord to which it could not belong, harmonically. In the analysis of passages with one or more pedals, the chords should be marked without reference to the pedal notes. The pedal can be indicated separately as in the examples below.

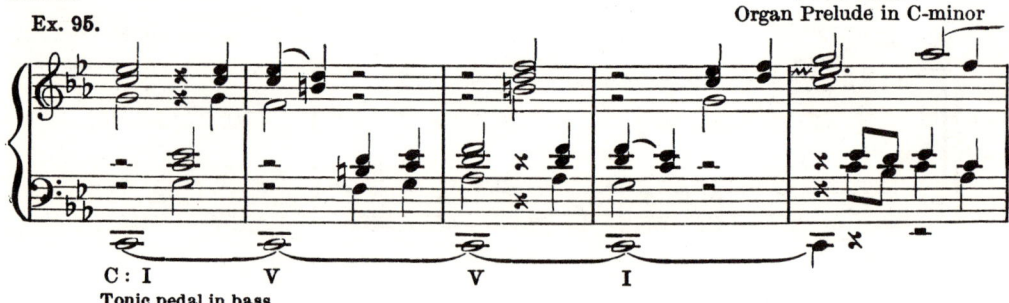

Ex. 95. J. S. Bach
Organ Prelude in C-minor

C: I   V   V   I

Tonic pedal in bass

Ex. 96.

Brahms. Op. 76, No. 4
Intermezzo

Rimsky-Korsakov
Scheherazade

Ex. 97.

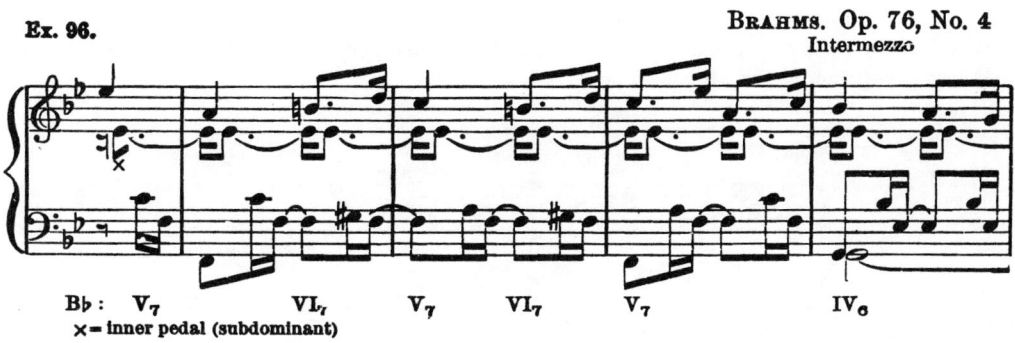

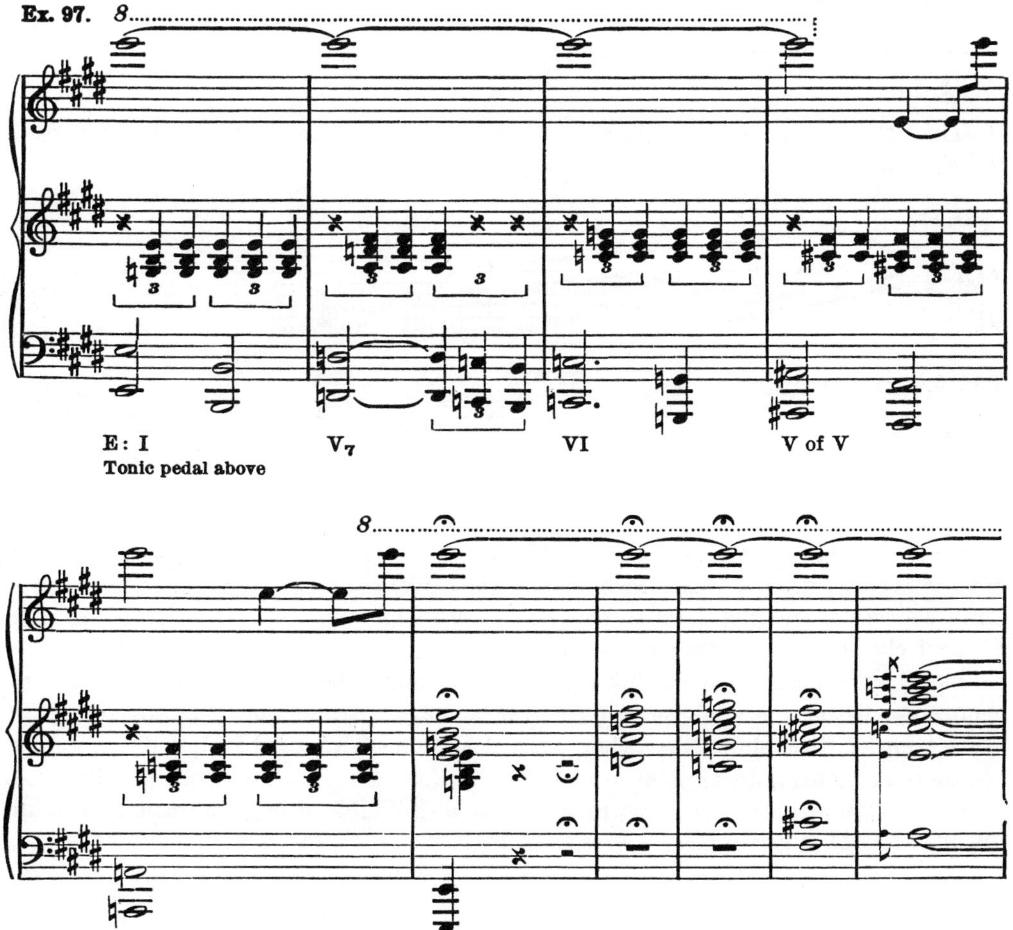

When a pedal note is foreign to but one chord in the passage, the effect may sometimes be analyzed in various ways. In the following very common example the explanations given below are all possible.

Ex. 98. MOZART
Sonata in F

a) Tonic pedal with V, I above.
b) I, with three appoggiature: g, e, and b-flat.
c) V, I with anticipation of tonic in the bass.
d) $\frac{V}{I}$, I.

The last indicates the presence of two harmonies at the same time, which often seems to be the case.

Ex. 99. BEETHOVEN. Op. 2, No. 2
Sonata

A: V $\frac{V}{I}$ I

All of the above analyses are preferable to calling the first of the two chords a chord of the eleventh on I. In fact, the chords of the eleventh and thirteenth, as well as most ninth chords (except the dominant ninth) do not come into common practice as independent chords until the time of Debussy.

As a general principle in this connection it might be stated that the fewer the chords the better the analysis will be from a musical standpoint. Naturally, in the application of this rule or any other, absurd extremes are possible, but if the student considers the contrapuntal point of view he will, for instance, notice that practically all cadential six-four chords are dominant chords with double appoggiatura, that the first inversion of III is in most cases V with a single appoggiatura, etc.

CHAPTER THREE

Modulation

Whatever the derivation and logic of the term may be, we understand modulation to mean change of key. In other words, it implies that the center of gravity of the music has changed, or is changing, and that the chords must be referred to a new tonic. For example, the triad, C – E – G may be considered to be I in the key of C. If, having so considered it, we then look upon it as being IV in G, we have modulated from the key of C to the key of G.

A change of tonality (synonymous with change of key) is a serious matter since it affects deeply the unity and variety of a piece of music. The determination of such changes presents one of the major problems of harmonic analysis and is far more important than finding the correct labels for the chords.

The first fact to be borne in mind is that the introduction of chromatic notes is not necessarily evidence of a modulation. One has only to look at the examples in chapter one to be convinced of this. Moreover, composers very often disregard correctness of notation in favor of an enharmonic spelling, which makes the chord easier to read for the performer.

Dvořák
Symphony No. 5
(Largo)

Ex. 100.

This passage should be written according to theory as follows:

Ex. 101.

D♭:   III   V₆ of II   III   I   VI   IV   I

The above example furnishes an excellent illustration of the alternation of chords from the minor and major modes in the same tonality. The first, third, fifth and sixth chords are derived from the minor mode, whereas the second, fourth and seventh chords are associated with the major mode.

The clearest type of modulation is that which is affirmed by a cadence in a new tonality. The cadence may be authentic, half, deceptive, or plagal.

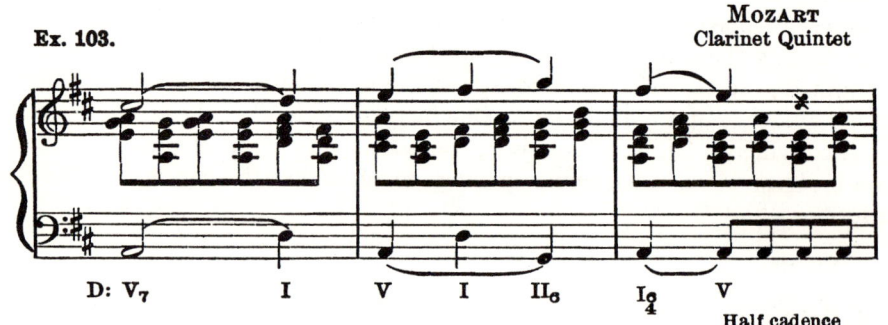

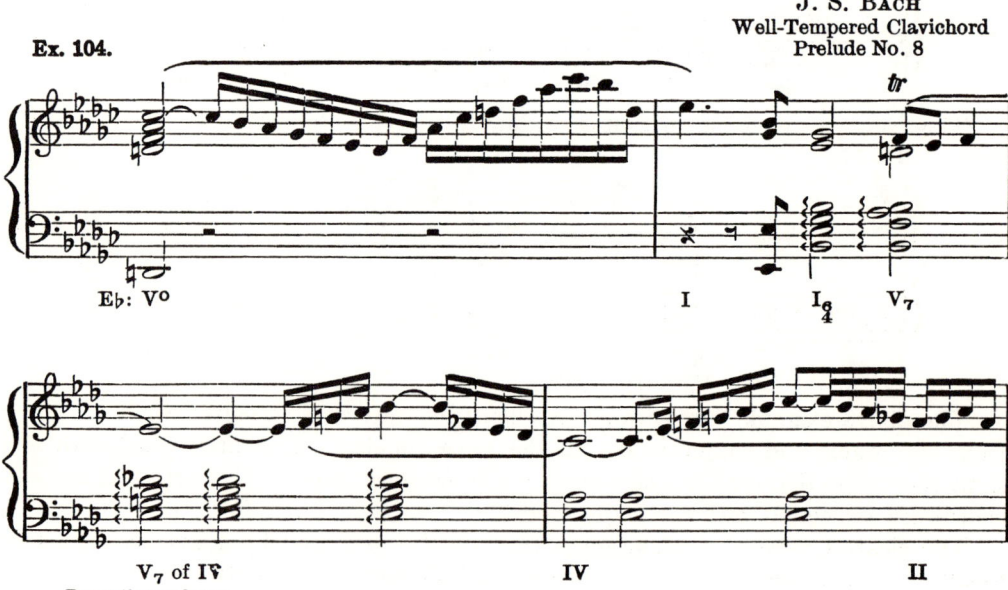

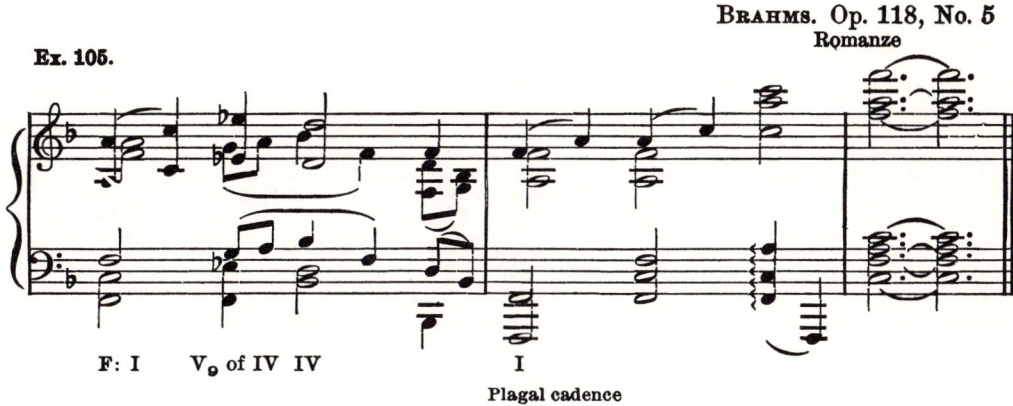

A half cadence may be confused with an authentic cadence denoting a modulation to the key of the dominant, in case the dominant chord in the cadence is preceded by V of V. If the next phrase begins in the original tonic key, one might say it would be pointless to consider a modulation to the dominant key. It should also be remembered that the six-four chord is one of the strongest tonal factors in a cadence, often forcing a modulation where it would be more logical to preserve the original tonality.

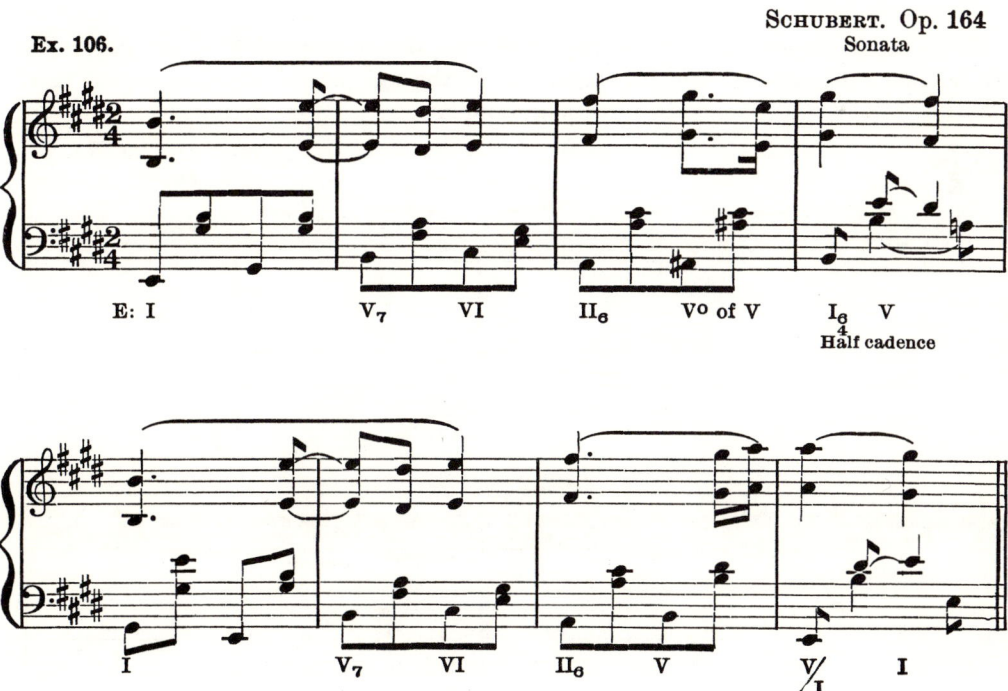

If the cadence shows a different key from that of the beginning of the phrase, it may happen that another key has been passed through before arriving at the final tonality. This would be termed a passing modulation.

MODULATION

The systematic transposition of a motive or group of chords usually results in a series of passing modulations, called a modulating sequence. Here it is usually more logical to observe the shifting tonalities rather than to analyze in fewer keys.

CHOPIN. Op. 28, No. 17
Prelude

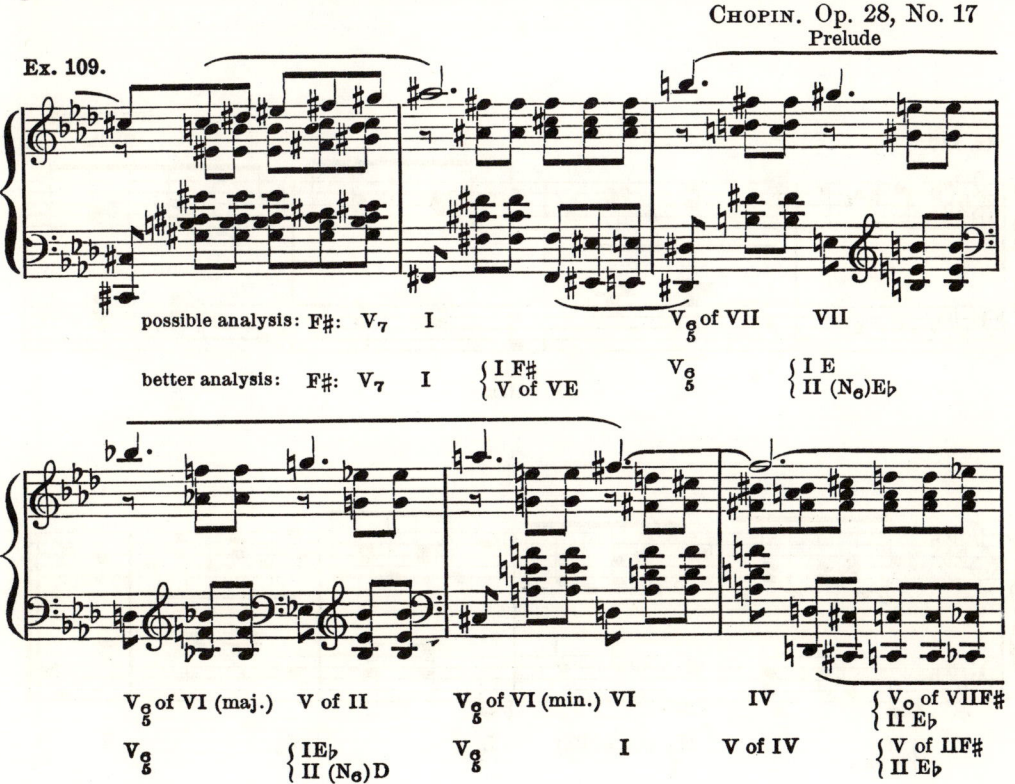

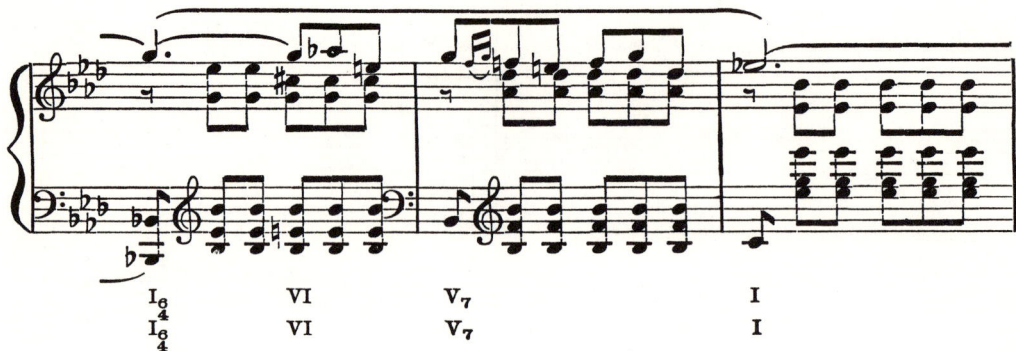

All of the chords in the above sequence can be explained in relation to the key of f-sharp, but this gives a forced interpretation, especially as compared to the symmetry and logic of the second analysis given.

Sometimes what seems to be a passing modulation is followed at once by a return to the original key. The term false modulation is applied to this procedure.

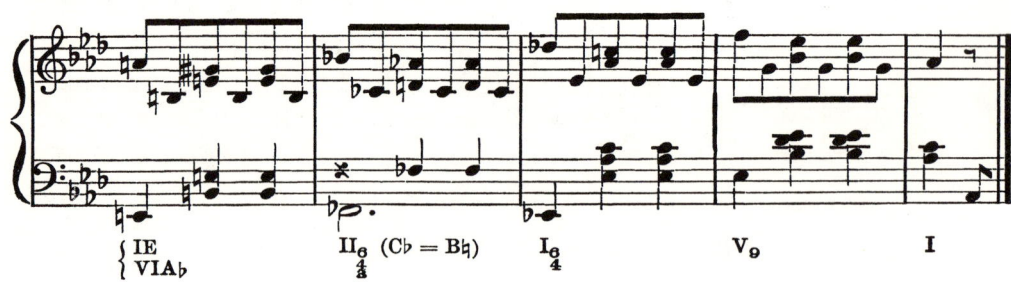

Although the use of such terms as II of IV, III of V, etc., would be stretching the bounds of tonality to perhaps an impossible extreme, there are many instances to be found in which the expression IV of V seems reasonable. In the following Brahms example, the subdominant chord in the fourth measure is preceded by its own subdominant (the g-minor chord) and the whole passage is quite definitely in a-minor.

Ex. 111. BRAHMS. Op. 51, No. 2

A: I   III   IV of IV   IV   V

Having determined that the music has modulated, the next problem is to find how and where the change may be said to have taken place. For the first of these questions this rule may be stated: Every modulation must be analyzed as arriving by means of a chord common to both keys, called the pivot chord.

A diatonic modulation is one in which the pivot chord is a chord without chromatic alteration in either key.

Ex. 112. BEETHOVEN. Op. 79 Sonata

G: I   V   { IG / VI B♭ }   I$_4^6$ V$_7$ I

A chromatic modulation is one in which the pivot chord is chromatically altered in one of the two keys or in both.

Ex. 113. FRANCK Symphony

D: V$_9$ of V   VI$_4^6$ V$_5^6$ of IV   IV$_7$ V° of V   V   { V$_9$ of VID / V$_9$B♭ }   I

Pivot chord altered in the first key   (deceptive cadence)

An enharmonic modulation is one in which the notation of the pivot chord requires enharmonic change to be correct for the second key or vice versa. It is obvious that in a modulation of this kind, it is unavoidable that the pivot chord should be incorrectly written for one key or the other. The composer usually adopts the notation which seems simplest for the reader.

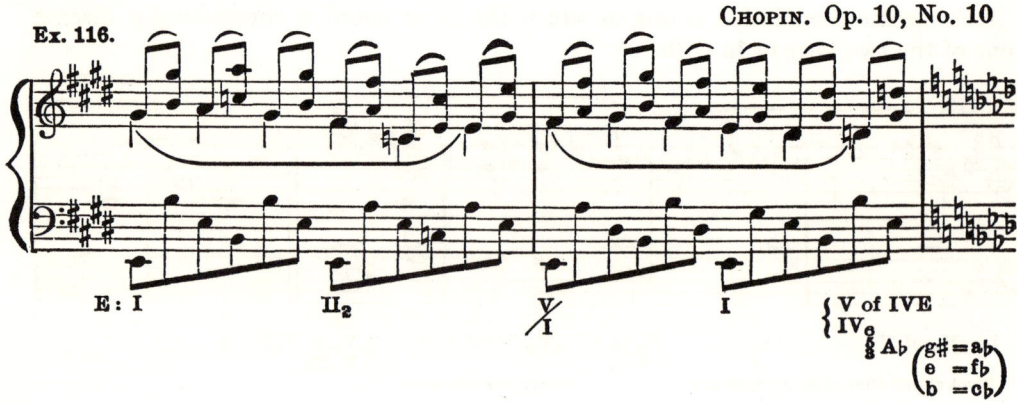

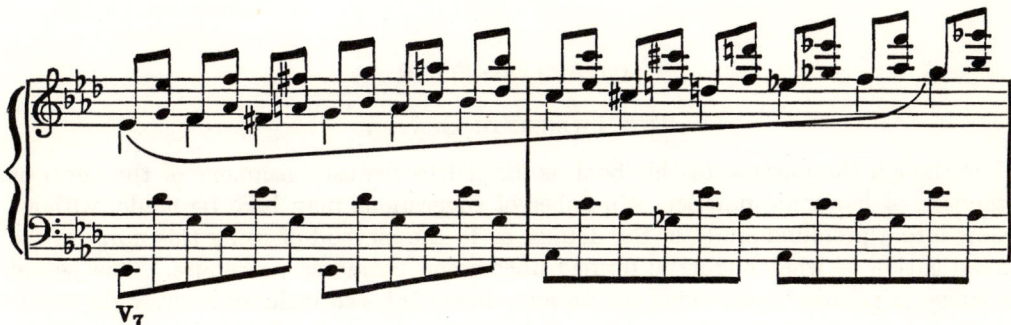

One often hears the expression — "change of key without modulation". If we mean by the term modulation a change of key, the expression is seen to be without logic. What is meant by it is that the modulation is very sudden and that no connection is apparent between the two keys. This may be acceptable as a description of the effect on the hearer, but cannot satisfy the musician, who is curious to know exactly what has happened technically. The simple process of explaining the last chord of the first key in terms of the second key will show just how weak, strong, or sudden the modulation may be.

The question of the location of the pivot chord is somewhat delicate and may be answered in part by saying that the composer modulates before the hearer. In other words, he has begun to look toward the new tonal center before he suggests his destination by the introduction of notes foreign to the first key. So the most reasonable position for the pivot chord would be at a point just before that at which characteristic harmonies of the new key are heard. This is often difficult to determine and, since some pairs of keys have many chords in common, there is often a choice of several possible pivot chords. The analyses of pieces in the appendix will furnish a variety of illustrations of this point.

CHAPTER FOUR

The Twentieth Century

Although the purpose of this book is limited to the establishment of the norm or standard of harmonic practice, a number of suggestions may here be made, without going into a profound study of the details, as to the method of using this norm in the investigation of what might be termed uncommon harmonic procedure. The period of common practice upon which the present theory is based includes roughly the eighteenth and nineteenth centuries, ending perhaps with the works of César Franck. There are throughout this period astonishingly few major differences in the material used and in the treatment of that material. The compositions of Sebastian Bach contain practically all the harmonic elements common at the time of Franck. It is not surprising, therefore, that one is bewildered by the number and variety of the new developments in the first quarter of the twentieth century.

One does not need to go to the music of the twentieth century to find composers breaking the rules. The bringing to light of the inevitable deviations from the commonplace on the part of every composer is perhaps the most interesting and profitable result to be obtained through harmonic analysis. These deviations not only play a large part in the composer's individual style, but contain the germs of the idioms of twentieth century composers. To the musical scholar falls the task of tracing the various lines of development to their sources, but it is also important for the practical musician to perceive that the process taking place is one of evolution and growth and distinctly not a simple rejection of the past.

Treatment of Harmonic Material

Considering the various elements of harmonic theory as we know it we begin most naturally with the uses of the triad. One notices at once a widespread tendency to use plain triads moving in similar motion (Puccini, *La Bohéme;* Chabrier, *Gwendoline;* Debussy, *La Cathédrale Engloutie*). Progressions hitherto forbidden become almost common. (II — I, Debussy, *La Demoiselle Elue;* V — IV with tritone, Fauré, *Clair de Lune.*) The use of the modal triads at the expense of those on the tonal degrees gives a pseudo-modal effect (Ravel, *Tombeau de Couperin*), while the whole-tone scale is necessarily bound up with successions of augmented triads. (Debussy, *Voiles.*) Triads in different keys, often used in succession over a pedal have enjoyed a certain vogue (Strauss, *Rosenkavalier*, motive of the rose).

With seventh chords there arises the question of the resolution of dissonance. In quest of freshness and novelty composers have tried all types of irregular resolutions, the most striking being perhaps that which results in parallel sevenths, or other dissonant intervals between the voices and complete abandonment of the resolution, as we are accustomed to think of it. (Ravel, Sonatina, minuet.) Notably in the works of

Fauré we find many charming and individual successions of seventh chords, hardly to be found in the works of any other composer.

The above remarks might be applied likewise to the chord of the ninth. This chord usually existed as a dominant, under accepted theory, but had already been resolved by similar motion in the César Franck Symphony, this device becoming the fashion twenty-five years later in American popular music. The popularity of the dominant major ninth amounted almost to an obsession early in the century and may be seen in exaggerated use in some of the sarabandes of Eric Satie. Ninth chords not in dominant form, as well as eleventh and thirteenth chords, may be found especially in music of the French composers. (Debussy, *Pelleas;* Ravel, *Valses Nobles et Sentimentales.*) Many experiments have been made with various chromatic alterations of these chords, resulting in effective and coloristic harmonies, especially when written for the orchestra (Ravel, *Daphnis et Chloe*).

Attempts have been made to construct chords by the use of other intervals than the third. Of these the only one which seems successful is the fourth. (Casella, Sonatina; Rebikov, "Album Leaf".) The difficulty is that the chords arrived at usually sound like some combination on a more familiar basis. For instance, a chord made of two fifths sounds like a ninth chord with third and seventh omitted. Both questions should interest the analyst, however. He should attempt to detect such a system on the part of the composer, but should at the same time scrutinize the result in its relation to the basic theory. It very often happens that the composer's ingenious imaginings produce an actual effect much nearer to the accepted line of development than he intended.

The intention on the part of the composer must, above all, be taken into account in considering those combinations of notes which are quite evidently used for their momentary sonority and color. (Honnegger, "Pacific 231".) There the relating of the various notes to a tonality or system is of use only for identification and classification and has little to do with explaining the actual effect, except in a negative way. Many examples may be found where chords of this type are used for their percussive effect alone. (Stravinsky, *Le Sacre du Printemps;* Bartók, Piano Sonata.)

Treatment of Contrapuntal Material

The employment of a complicated system of non-harmonic tones over a simple and conventional harmonic basis was a favorite device among German composers of the late nineteenth century and accounts for some of the apparent complexities in the scores of Richard Strauss. Composers soon discovered that voices moving chromatically may be combined almost at random, using the principle of the chromatic passing tone to such an extent that the underlying chord is sometimes never actually heard. This must be differentiated from the use of chromatic counterpoint without reference to chords, although both result in a somewhat invertebrate kind of music.

The most important development in connection with the treatment of non-harmonic tones is probably the rapid acceleration taking place in the evolution of the principle of the non-resolution of dissonances, such as the appoggiatura and the suspension. This principle may be said to exist to a greater or less degree in the general practice of all modern composers. (Bartók, *Quatre Nénies*, final cadence.) The unresolved appoggiatura or suspension is often heard at the same time with its note of resolution (Hindemith, *das Marienleben*, final cadence), and if the idea is carried out consistently polytonality will result (Ravel, Piano Concerto).

Another possible source of polytonality is the elaboration of the pedal. Two harmonies are heard simultaneously whenever the pedal, instead of being a single tone, is a chord or ostinato figure (Honnegger, *Le Roi David;* Holst, "Dirge for Two Veterans").

Tonality and Modality

The presence of a center of gravity, or tonic, being the sole requisite for the presence of a tonality, it will be seen that the same tonality may be given a large number of variations in the make-up of its scale. The major and minor modes on the same tonic are practically interchangeable according to our theory, and, after Chopin, Wagner and Franck, might be thought of as being absorbed into a chromatic scale or mode, retaining the original tonic, dominant, and subdominant. As a relief from this excess of chromaticism we find many composers adopting a modified form of the old church modes (Pizzetti, Respighi), or of those to be found in folk-song (Vaughan-Williams, Holst). Some of the latter being of oriental derivation sound strange and novel to our ears and should obviously not be explained by reference to our major and minor limitations (Kodaly, Bartók, Stravinsky).

Experiments have also been made with the artificial construction of scales. The whole-tone scale, dividing the octave into six equal parts, exploited by Debussy and his followers, had an extraordinary vogue in view of the little it had to offer in organic life and variety. The imposing number of new scales proposed by Busoni shows the speculative possibilities in this direction.

Polytonality and Atonality

The conscious combination of two or more strands of music in different keys sounding simultaneously has shown that, while two keys can be heard, the employment of several defeats its own end and destroys the feeling of any tonality. (Stravinsky, Milhaud, Honnegger.) Even with only two keys, the adjustment must be delicately made if the ear is to be prevented from absorbing the whole into one main tonality. The usual method is to use keys an augmented fourth apart (as C and F-sharp), these having fewer notes in common than any other pair. Polytonal writing is most successful in the orchestra where different planes of tone-color or dynamics may be used.

Atonality, or absence of tonality, is usually connected with the music of Schoenberg, whose highly developed theories should be studied in detail before an intelligent analysis of his works or of those of his disciples can be made. If there is to be no tonality, or center of gravity, it means that no degree of the scale shall assume more importance than the others — a condition difficult of realization for any length of time. Short passages may be found even in Chopin where the key is distinctly indeterminate, but all music has sooner or later to come to a cadence of some form and it is here that the balance of power between the notes is apt to be lost. The atonal idiom has been used effectively by a large proportion of twentieth century composers and is desirable as an increase in technical resources, but should not be expected to supplant existing idioms.

Various Styles

The technical styles employed by composers can be grouped into four general classes; the purely contrapuntal, the purely harmonic, the combined harmonic and contrapuntal, and the purely rhythmic.

For the first of these we often hear the slogan, "back to Bach." This is inaccurate, inasmuch as Bach was a soundly harmonic composer. The "back to Bach" movement, so-called, was more a return to the point of view of counterpoint without reference to chords and is well exemplified in the works of Hindemith and Toch. The type of melodic line employed by these men explains the reference to Bach. Schoenberg and Berg are also in the contrapuntal tradition, although with a different melodic approach. It is unavoidable that counterpoint should make chords, but one should appreciate the fact that here the harmony is a by-product of more important considerations.

Purely harmonic writing is rarely used for whole pieces, although the kaleidoscopic movement in Schoenberg's Five Orchestral Pieces is a famous example. The usual procedure is a combination of the harmonic and contrapuntal. Even the exponents of the contrapuntal and atonal idioms sometimes write chords. The rhythmic style, or the reduction of the music to rhythm alone may be seen in some pages of the *Sacre du Printemps* and in many of the later works of Béla Bartók. It is necessary to add a reminder that the imitation of sounds other than music has always tempted composers. In Mossolov's "Iron Foundry" and some of Varese's scores a tremendous sonority is built up for its own sake. The opposite is found in the miniature orchestral pieces of von Webern.

The foregoing remarks are intended merely as hints or suggestions for a plan of investigation into a field which would need at least a volume to study. It is evident that the expression "common practice" can no longer be applied. The divergent practices, however, may be intelligently scrutinized and appreciated by relating them to the main principle, the foundation of common practice which it is hoped this book provides.

APPENDIX

Examples of Complete Harmonic Analysis of Pieces

1. BACH: Prelude No. 1, from the "Well-Tempered Clavichord"
2. BACH: Choral ("*Christus ist erstanden*")
3. BACH: Sarabande, from English Suite No. 1
4. HAYDN: Minuetto, from String Quartet — Op. 76, No. 3
5. MOZART: Andante (first section) from Sonata in F
6. BEETHOVEN: Scherzo (first part) from Sonata — Op. 2, No. 3
7. SCHUMANN: Romance — Op. 28, No. 2
8. CHOPIN: Prelude — Op. 29, No. 3
9. BRAHMS: Intermezzo — Op. 119, No. 1
10. FRANCK: Fragment from String Quartet (Third Movement)

Abbreviations used in the Analysis

ant.	anticipation
app.	appoggiatura
aux.	auxiliary
camb.	cambiata
db. aux.	double auxiliary
éch.	échappée
pt.	passing-tone
ped.	pedal
susp.	suspension

1. Prelude Nº I
From the "Well-Tempered Clavichord"

Johann Sebastian Bach
(1685-1750)

(1) The C might be accounted for as a suspension resolving in the next measure.

(2) This seems the most natural location for the pivot chord since it is just before the dominant seventh of the new key.

E.C.S. Nº 757

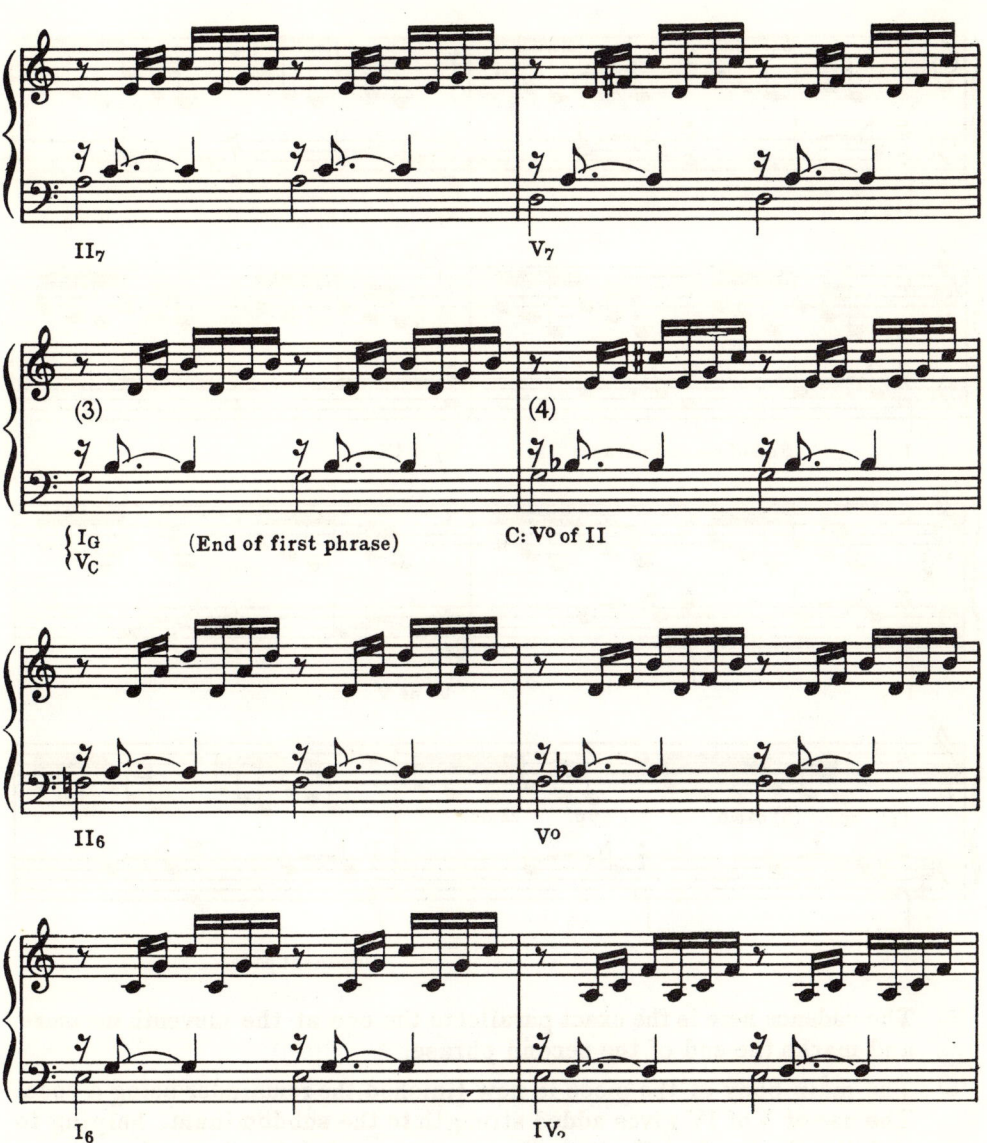

(3) This and the two preceding measures give the first sign of cadential formula strong enough to mark the end of a phrase. The chief factors are the movement of the bass and the choice of the chords II, V, and I in root position.

(4) A passing modulation through D might be indicated here, but seems unnecessary since this chord is very common in the key of C.

E.C.S. No. 757

(5) The cadence here is the exact parallel to the one at the eleventh measure, and marks the end of the second phrase.

(6) The main body of the piece is now finished, the remainder being a coda. The use of V of IV gives added strength to the subdominant, helping to stabilize the key by offsetting the previous modulation to the dominant.

(7) Many editions contain an interpolated measure before this one, a passing tonic six-four chord. It was probably inserted to avoid cross relations F-sharp to F-natural and A-natural to A-flat. This in itself not only weakens the harmony but the introduction of the dominant bass destroys all the effect of Bach's approach to the dominant pedal.

(8) An interpretation of the B as a note of the harmony would likewise involve an anticlimax. The harmony must be heard and played as II introducing V.

(9) It is evident that the chromatic movement in the tenor would more naturally be written D, D-sharp, E.

E.C.S. No 757

2. Choral
("Christus ist erstanden")

JOHANN SEBASTIAN BACH
(1685-1750)

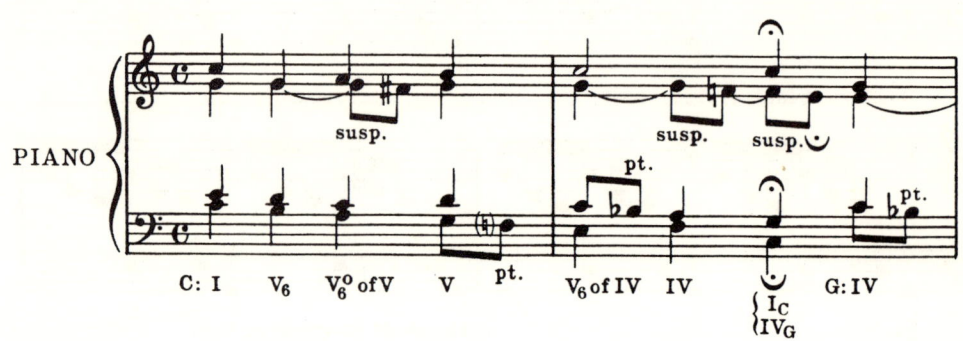

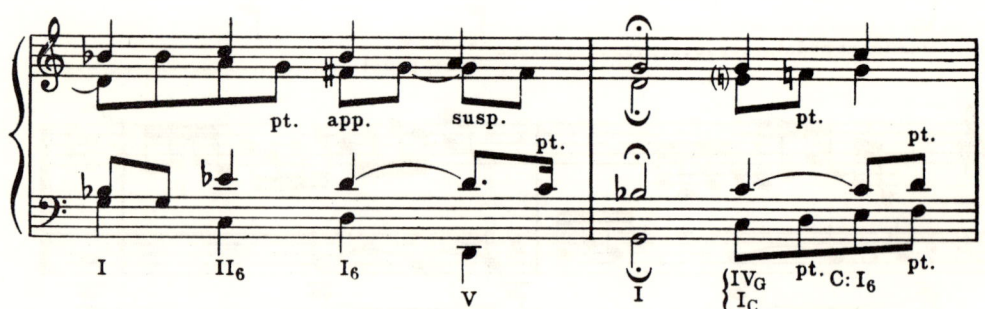

(1) The E may be regarded as a suspension resolving upward.

(2) The use of so much of the key of B-flat causes the final cadence to sound as a half cadence in F. Indeed the distribution of keys as shown by the analysis is distinctly to the disadvantage of the tonality of C.

E.C.S. No. 757

3. Sarabande
From English Suite № 1

JOHANN SEBASTIAN BACH
(1685-1750)

(1) It would perhaps be more accurate to interpret the first D as an anticipation of the appoggiatura, with E as auxiliary between.

(2) The presence of the inverted mordant gives this B more rhythmical importance than it would otherwise have, hence its classification as appoggiatura rather than passing-tone.

(3) The B in the upper voice is interpolated between the dissonance A and its resolution G-sharp, and so has the contrapuntal characteristics of the échappée, even though it happens to coincide with a note of the chord.

(4) Notice the change from six-part to four-part writing, and later on to three.

(5) The suspension resolves after the harmony changes.

E.C.S. № 757

(6) These three notes being rhythmically alike, it seems logical to name them alike, a B being understood before the A-sharp.

(7) As in the first measure, the first of the two thirty-second notes may be the more important, in which case it should be called an appoggiatura.

(8) The D would normally progress to C-sharp making the dominant seventh. An interpretation as an unresolved appoggiatura is always preferable to calling this combination a thirteenth chord.

(9) The E resolves to D, with interpolated échappée F-sharp. This in turn, is introduced by the cambiata G. Harmonically the chord IV results but the contrapuntal origin is interesting.

E.C.S. No. 757

4. Minuetto
From String Quartet

JOSEF HAYDN. Op. 76, No 3
(1732-1809)

(1) The simplicity of this music is striking when compared with the Bach *Sarabande*. The analysis of the classics is always without difficulty if one has studied thoroughly much of Bach.

(2) These chords coming on the beat and resolving by step may be explained as two, three, or even four appoggiature.

E.C.S. No 757

64

(3) The harmonic explanation of the first beat as VI, IV or even II is possible.

E.C.S. № 757

5. Sonata in F
(Andante—first section)

Wolfgang Amadeus Mozart
(1756-1791)

(1) The use of the dominant major ninth with root is not common in music of the eighteenth century, except when the ninth occurs as a suspension or other non-harmonic note.

(2) The missing root of this chord in F would be D (V of II), whereas in E-flat it would be F (V of V). The diminished seventh chord is a vague chord, with many enharmonic possibilities, its orientation being determined by the identity of its missing root. The extent of these possibilities may be appreciated by going through the list of chords in Chapter One and noting those which have the form of the diminished seventh chord and which have the same sound, enharmonically.

(3) A false modulation to E-flat, caused by the tonal strength of the six-four chord. This chord is difficult of assimilation into the key of F, hence the modulation.

6. Sonata
(Scherzo—first part)

LUDWIG VAN BEETHOVEN. Op. 2, No. 3
(1770-1827)

(1) Although there is only the one melodic line as evidence, the dominant harmony progressing to the tonic is plainly heard.

(2) It is characteristic of Beethoven that he should be content with so many repetitions of V-I. The surprising fact is that no lack of harmonic variety is felt in this movement.

E.C.S. No. 757

72

(3) The formula V-I still persists, but passing through different keys.

E.C.S. No. 757

(4) The return of the first theme is here marked, not by change of harmony but by the sudden introduction of the major sixth degree, after the minor has been reiterated seven times.

(5) This piece illustrates the interchange between major and minor forms on the same tonic. It is in C-major and not C-minor for the sole reason that the balance of power remains with the major third degree.

7. Romance

Robert Schumann. Op. 28, No 2
(1810-1856)

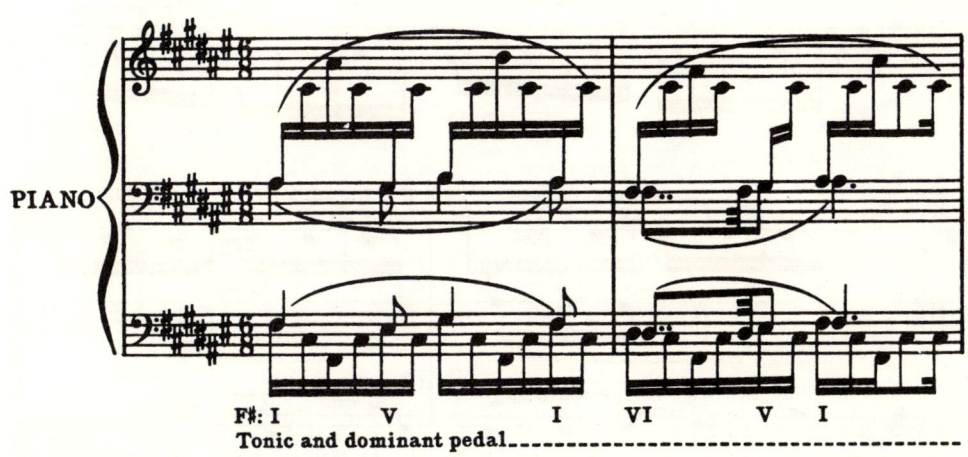

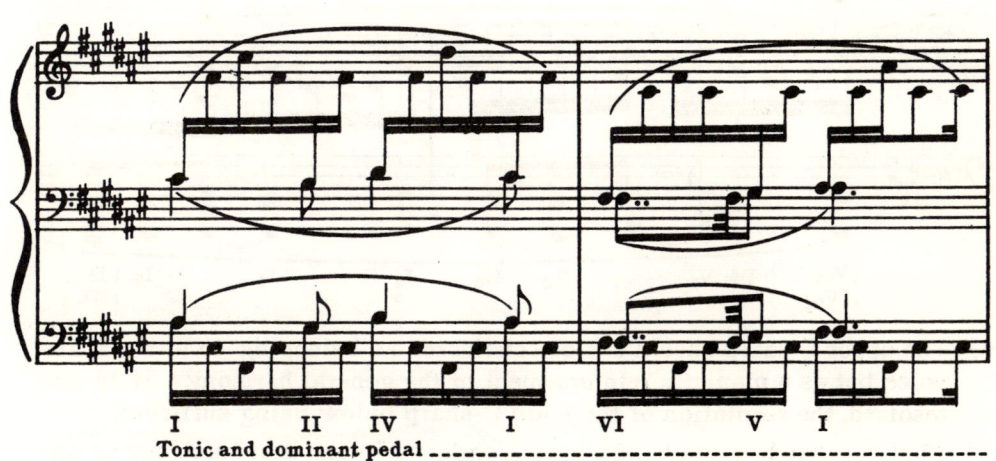

E.C.S. No 757

76

(1) The upper C-sharp should not be considered as belonging to a separate voice but as a pianistic reinforcement of the general harmony. It is not resolved, the resolution of the main C-sharp below being sufficent.

(2) This is a good example of a strong cadence in the dominant key as opposed to a half cadence in the tonic key. The six-four chord on the strong beat is the most characteristic.

(3) A modulating sequence of two-measure pattern. The symmetry of the music should be matched by symmetry in the analysis.

(4) This sequence of diminished seventh harmonies seems vague and wandering at first, but if studied will prove to be modulating systematically downward by fifths. The somewhat carefree notation employed by the composer is an added difficulty to a realization of the correct roots.

(5) Ordinarily this six-four chord would indicate a modulation to G but this is counteracted by the presence of C-sharp in a prominent place.

E.C.S. No. 757

78

(6) Deceptive cadence.

E.C.S. No. 757

(7) A beautiful example of extended cadence.

(8) Coda in the form of an extension of the final chord.

(9) This unorthodox use of the six-four chord for ending gives a feeling of suspense and indefiniteness impossible with the chord in root position.

E. C. S. № 757

8. Prélude

FRÉDÉRIC CHOPIN. Op. 29, No. 3
(1810-1849)

(1) Half cadence, end of the first phrase.
(2) This shifting of the tonality, with strong triad progressions, is a familiar device in the music of Wagner and as used here by Chopin leads one into remote keys.

E.C.S. No 757

(3) The six-four chord of A-flat with consequent authentic cadence is the distant objective of the second phrase, but this proves to be, enharmonically, the third degree of E, so the return is simple.

(4) This return to the home key is very sudden and like a burst of light. Chopin has indicated a big *crescendo* to *fortissimo* in order to make sure of his effect.

E.C.S. No. 757

9. Intermezzo

JOHANNES BRAHMS. Op. 119, No. 7
(1833-1897)

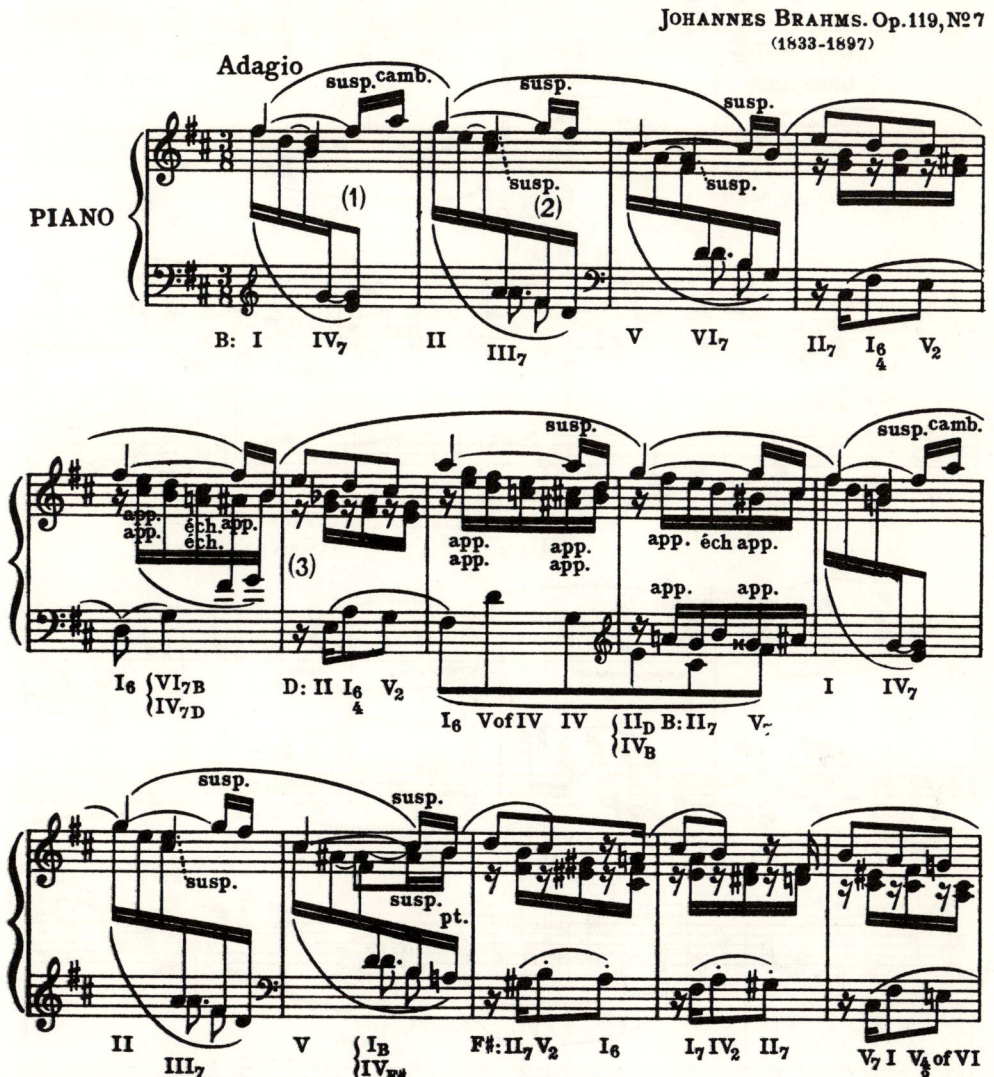

(1) The F-sharp would normally resolve to E but here has an upward resolution, ornamented by a cambiata.
(2) In actual performance the E disappears when the D below is struck, this taking the place of a resolution.
(3) False modulation to D.

E.C.S. No. 757

(4) The appoggiatura A-sharp has an ornamental resolution, by striking a note of the chord, F-sharp, before its note of resolution, B.

E.C.S. No 757

(5) The suspended notes A and F-sharp are, despite the rests, resolved to G and E.

(6) This suspension passes through a chromatic passing tone to an upward resolution.

E.C.S. No 757

10. Fragment from String Quartet
(Third Movement)

CÉSAR FRANCK
(1822-1890)

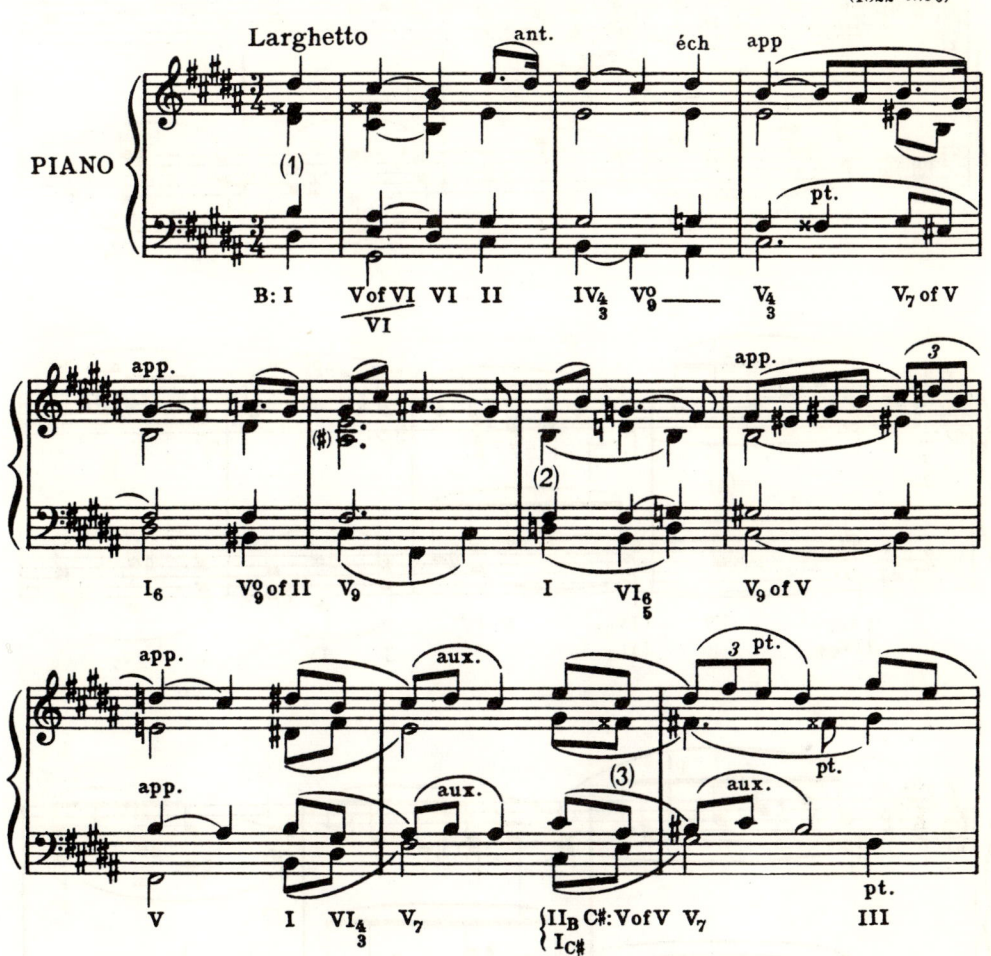

(1) The whole phrase sounds like G-sharp-minor up to the cadence (last chord in third full measure to first chord in fourth). The cadence, however, indicates the key of the phrase, unless the chords are incapable of analysis in that key. It will be noticed that these are all good chords in the key of B, so that the allusion to G-sharp-minor is a subtlety.

(2) Note the oscillation between major and minor modes of B.

(3) These three measures are characteristic of the chromaticism of Franck.

E.C.S. Nº 757

88

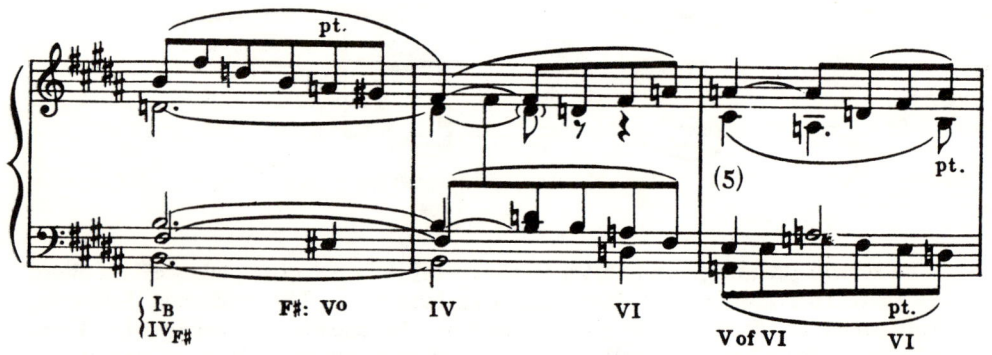

(4) There is a slight feeling of modality here with a center, C-sharp.

(5) A strong allusion to D-major but not enough to force a modulation.

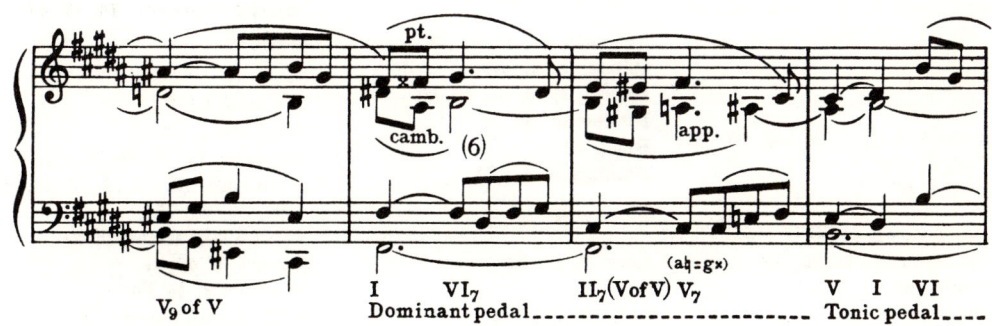

(6) One should notice that the **tonic** six-four chord is strongly felt throughout the measure. The sixth degree can rarely have the force of a real harmonic root unless it is in the bass. The G-sharp might reasonably be considered an appoggiatura without resolution, the "added sixth," spoken of by theorists as far back as Rameau.

INDEX

abbreviations, 53
accented passing-tone, 31
anticipation, 36
appoggiatura, 31, 34
atonality, 50
augmented six-five-three, 19
augmented six-four-three, 11, 23
augmented sixth, 19
authentic cadence, 40, 42
auxiliary tone, 35

Bach, J. S., 13, 15, 18, 27, 30, 33, 34, 35, 36, 40, 48, 54, 58, 60
Bach, W. F., 12
Bartók, 49, 50, 51
Beethoven, 4, 8, 19, 20, 22, 28, 31, 32, 38, 45, 51, 71
Berg, 51
Berlioz, 8
Bizet, 12
Brahms, 3, 5, 8, 24, 26, 37, 41, 45, 46, 83
Busoni, 50

cadences, 41, 42, 43
cambiata, 33, 34, 35, 36
Casella, 49
Chabrier, 48
Chopin, 4, 10, 15, 19, 34, 36, 42, 43, 46, 81
chords on the dominant, 20
" " " mediant, 12
" " " seventh degree, 27
" " " subdominant, 16
" " " submediant, 23
" " " supertonic, 7
" " " tonic, 2
chromatic modulation, 45
Couperin, 12

Debussy, 38, 48, 49, 50
deceptive cadence, 40
diatonic modulation, 45
dominant chords, 20

dominants on all degrees, 1
dominants without root, 1, 6, 27
double auxiliary, 36
doubly-augmented fourth, 11
Dvórak, 39

échappée, 33, 34, 35, 36
eleventh chords, 38, 49
enharmonic modulation, 46

false modulation, 44
Fauré, 48, 49
Franck, 7, 9, 17, 20, 34, 35, 45, 48, 49, 87

Grieg, 9, 23, 26

half cadence, 40, 41, 42
Händel, 3, 27, 86
Haydn, 7, 10, 20, 40, 63
Hindemith, 50, 51
Holst, 50
Honnegger, 49, 50

Kodaly, 50

Liszt, 7, 17, 22
Lalo, 21
lowered fifth, 23

Mattheson, 29
mediant chords, 12
Mendelssohn, 27, 33
Milhaud, 50
modality, 50
modulating sequence, 43
modulation, 39
Moussorgsky, 28, 29
Mossolov, 51
Mozart, 2, 6, 14, 16, 18, 23, 30, 32, 38, 40, 42, 66

Neapolitan sixth, 12, 26
ninth chords, 4, 38, 49
non-harmonic tones, 30, 49

passing modulation, 42
passing-tone, 30
pedal, 36, 37, 38
pivot chord, 4o
Pizzetti, 50
plagal cadence, 4'
polytonality, 50
Puccini, 48
Purcell, 24

raised fifth, 22
Rameau, 25
Ravel, 48, 49, 50
Rebikov, 49
Respighi, 50
Rimsky-Korsakov, 14, 17, 37
Rust, 28

Satie, 49
Scarlatti, 21, 33
Schoenberg, 50, 51
Schubert, 11, 19, 25, 26, 41, 44
Schumann, 13, 14, 16, 18, 21, 25, 29, 32, 46, 75
seventh degree chords, 27
Strauss, 5, 48, 49
Stravinsky, 49, 50
subdominant chords, 16
submediant chords, 23
supertonic chords, 7
suspension, 32, 34

Tchaikovsky, 11
thirteenth chords, 38, 49
tonality, 50
tonic chords, 2
Toch, 51

Varese, 51
Vaughan-Williams, 50

Wagner, 3, 13, 15, 16, 24, 31, 47
Weber, 6
Webern, 51

The Concord Series

of Music and Books on the Teaching of Music

Under the editorship of Dr. Thomas Whitney Surette and Archibald T. Davison, Ph.D., F.R.C.M., Mus.D.

No.		
1	25 Chorals by Johann Sebastian Bach. Elsmith *and* Surette (*See also Nos. 615 and 1799*) Cloth 1.50 Paper	1.25
2	The Home and Community Song Book with Piano Accompaniment. Davison *and* Surette (*See also No. 19, Vocal Edition*) Complete Edition Boards	2.00
3	140 Folk-Songs. Rote Songs for Grades I, II and III (Words and Melodies only) Davison *and* Surette (*See also No. 7, Teachers' Edition*) New large-note Students' Edition Cloth	1.35
4	A Book of Songs for Unison and Part Singing. For Grades IV, V and VI (Words and Melodies only) Davison, Surette *and* Zanzig (*See also No. 14, Teachers' Edition*) Students' Edition Cloth	1.80
5	Twenty Marches for use in Schools. Edited by Thomas Whitney Surette	1.25
6	The Concord Teachers' Guide (*A Manual for all Grades*) by Augustus D. Zanzig	.50
7	140 Folk-Songs with Piano Accompaniment. Rote Songs for Grades I, II and III. Davison *and* Surette (*See also No. 3, Students' Edition*) Teachers' Edition Cloth	2.50
8	Robin Hood (*A Play with music for Children*) by Kate Stearns Page	.75
9	A Kindergarten Book of Folk-Songs. Lorraine d'Oremieulx Warner Cloth	2.50
10	The Concord Hymnal for Day School, Sunday School and Home. Katherine Huntington *and* Elizabeth MacLaren Robinson Cloth	1.50
11	The Nativity (*A Play for Children, with music founded on Old French Songs*) by Lorraine d'Oremieulx Warner *and* Margaret Higginson Barney	.75
12	Principles of Musical Theory by Renée Longy-Miquelle Cloth	2.00
13	The Concord Anthem Book (40 Anthems) For Mixed Voice Choirs in Protestant Churches. Davison *and* Foote (*See also Nos. 1200 and 1290*) Cloth	2.50
14	A Book of Songs with Piano Accompaniment (For Unison and Part Singing for Grades IV, V and VI) Davison, Surette *and* Zanzig (*See also No. 4, Students' Edition*) Teachers' Edition Cloth	4.00
15	Concord Junior Song and Chorus Book with Piano Accompaniment (Boys and Girls) For Unison and Part Singing for Grades VII, VIII and IX. Davison, Surette *and* Zanzig (*See also No. 16, Students' Edition*) Teachers' Edition Cloth	5.00
16	Concord Junior Song and Chorus Book (Boys and Girls) For Unison and Part Singing for Grades VII, VIII and IX (Words and Voice Parts only) Davison, Surette *and* Zanzig (*See also No. 15, Teachers' Edition*) Students' Edition Cloth	2.50
17	Concord Song Book for Women's Voices with Piano Accompaniment. Davison *and* Surette (*See also No. 18, Students' Edition*) Teachers' Edition Cloth	5.00
18	Concord Song Book for Women's Voices (Words and Voice Parts only) Davison *and* Surette (*See also No. 17, Teachers' Edition*) Students' Edition Cloth	2.50
19	The Home and Community Song Book (Words and Voice Parts only) Davison *and* Surette (*See also No. 2, Complete Edition*) Vocal Edition Cloth	1.25
50 / 100 / 1000 / 1050 / 1100 / 1400	Harvard University Glee Club Collection of Part Songs for Men's Voices. Everlastingly the best collection in the world of the finest choral music for Men's Voices. *Compiled and Arranged by* Archibald T. Davison. Six Volumes Cloth each Special Library offer for one set of six volumes $12.00	3.00
601	The Concord Piano Books. Elementary Course of Instruction, based on Folk-songs (with words) and on Physical Interpretation of Rhythm by Katherine K. Davis (Four Volumes) Vol. I	1.25
602	Vol. II	1.25
603	Vol. III	1.35
604	Vol. IV	1.35
605	Béla Bartók Album of Selected Pieces for the Piano. *Compiled by* Katherine K. Davis (Two Volumes) Vol. I	1.00
606	Vol. II	1.00
607	Themes from the Masters. *Simply arranged for Piano, four hands,* by Faith Cabot Pigors	1.25
608	The Concord Duet Book for First Sight-Playing (*Based on Folk-tunes*) by Katherine K. Davis	1.00
610	The Headless Horseman (*An Operetta in One Act for High Schools*) based on Washington Irving's *A Legend of Sleepy Hollow*. Libretto by Stephen Vincent Benét. Music by Douglas Moore. (Orchestration available) Paper	2.50
611	Concord Classics for the Piano (*Compositions of the 16th, 17th and 18th Centuries*) *Compiled by* Willi Apel Paper	1.50
615	Second Book of Chorals (28) by Johann Sebastian Bach. Edited and provided with suitable English texts by Thomas Whitney Surette (*See also Nos. 1 and 1799*) Cloth 1.50 Paper	1.25
616	Cinderella (*A Folk-tune Operetta in Three Acts, without spoken dialogue*) by Katherine K. Davis	.75
617	Six and Four are Ten (*A Play with music and dancing, based on an Old Welsh Fairy Tale*) by Ursula Ridley	.75
618 / 619	The Wellesley Appreciation Album for the Piano (*Characteristic Selections from the Music of Great Composers*) *Compiled by* Edward Barry Greene (Volumes I and II) Paper each Cloth each	2.00 3.50
1200	Second Concord Anthem Book (40 Anthems) For Mixed Voice Choirs in Protestant Churches. Davison *and* Foote (*See also Nos. 13 and 1290*) Cloth	2.50
1290	Third Concord Anthem Book (30 Anthems) For Mixed Voice Choirs in Protestant Churches. Victoria Glaser *and* Henry Clough-Leighter (*See also Nos. 13 and 1200*) Cloth	2.50
1799	Third Book of Chorals (25) by Johann Sebastian Bach. Edited and provided with suitable English texts by Henry Clough-Leighter (*See also Nos. 1 and 615*) Cloth 1.50 Paper	1.25
2159	Fourth Concord Anthem Book (20 Anthems) For Male Voice Choirs in Protestant Churches. Victor H. Mattfeld *and* Henry Clough-Leighter (*See also No. 2160*) Boards *in press*	
2160	Fifth Concord Anthem Book (20 Anthems) For Male Voice Choirs in Protestant Churches. Victor H. Mattfeld *and* Henry Clough-Leighter (*See also No. 2159*) Boards *in press*	

(*Prices subject to change without notice*)

A complete, descriptive catalog of the works of The Concord Series is available gratis upon request.

E. C. SCHIRMER MUSIC COMPANY
221 Columbus Ave., Boston 16, Mass.

JAN 3 1 1993

DATE DUE			
JUL - 8 1993			
GAYLORD			PRINTED IN U.S.A.